Developing New Services

Incorporating the Voice of the Customer into Strategic Service Development

Also available from ASQ Quality Press:

From Quality to Business Excellence: A Systems Approach to Management
Charles G. Cobb

Customer Centered Six Sigma: Linking Customers, Process Improvement, and Financial Results
Earl Naumann and Steven H. Hoisington

Customer Satisfaction Measurement Simplified: A Step-by-Step Guide for ISO 9001:2000 Certification
Terry G. Vavra

The Trust Imperative: Performance Improvement through Productive Relationships
Stephen Hacker and Marsha Willard

Office Kaizen: Transforming Office Operations into a Strategic Competitive Advantage
William Lareau

Analysis of Customer Satisfaction Data
Derek R. Allen and Tanniru R. Rao

Measuring Customer Satisfaction: Survey Design, Use, and Statistical Analysis Methods, Second Edition
Bob E. Hayes

Improving Your Measurement of Customer Satisfaction: A Guide to Creating, Conducting, Analyzing, and Reporting Customer Satisfaction Measurement Programs
Terry G. Vavra

Developing New Services

Incorporating the Voice of the Customer into Strategic Service Development

Caroline M. Fisher
James T. Schutta

ASQ Quality Press
Milwaukee, Wisconsin

American Society for Quality, Quality Press, Milwaukee 53203

Printed in the United States of America

12 11 10 09 08 07 06 05 04 03 5 4 3 2 1

Library of Congress Cataloging-in-Publication Data

Fisher, Caroline M., 1947–
Developing new services : incorporating the voice of the customer into strategic service development / Caroline M. Fisher and James T. Schutta.
p. cm.
Includes bibliographical references and index.
ISBN 0-87389-585-1 (Hard cover, case binding : alk. paper)
1. Customer services—Management. 2. Customer services—Quality control. 3. Service industries—Management. 4. Service industries—Quality control. 5. Consumer satisfaction—Statistical methods. I. Schutta, James T., 1944– II. Title.

HF5415.5F565 2003
658.8'12—dc21 2003005130

ISBN 0-87389-585-1

Publisher: William A. Tony
Acquisitions Editor: Annemieke Koudstaal
Project Editor: Paul O'Mara
Production Administrator: Gretchen Trautman
Special Marketing Representative: David Luth

Printed on acid-free paper

American Society for Quality
ASQ®

Quality Press
600 N. Plankinton Avenue
Milwaukee, Wisconsin 53203
Call toll free 800-248-1946
Fax 414-272-1734
www.asq.org
http://qualitypress.asq.org
http://standardsgroup.asq.org
E-mail: authors@asq.org

We dedicate this book to our spouses, Daryl and Mary Jane, who kept us focused throughout the long hours of making our dream a reality.

Table of Contents

List of Figures and Tables . . . . *xi*

Preface . . . . *xv*

Chapter 1 Introduction **1**

Services 3

Internal Services 4

QFD for Services 4

The Purpose of This Book 5

Chapter 2 Voice of the Customer and Quality Function Deployment Overview **9**

Part I Voice of the Customer

Chapter 3 Understanding Consumer Choice Decisions **17**

Attributes and Consequences 18

Compensatory Decision-Making Model 20

The Doctor's Office 23

Exercises 24

Chapter 4 Voice of the Customer **25**

Interviews 26

Focus Groups 27

The Modified Kano Model 28

Other Sources of Data 31

Organizing the Customer Voice 32

Finding and Adding Missing Consequences 34

The Doctor's Office 35

Exercise 35

Chapter 5 The Importance of Importance 37
Importance Ratings 38
Basics of Measurement 39
Alternative Importance Scales 41
The Doctor's Office 44
Exercise 45

Chapter 6 Customer Competitive Analysis 47
Competitive Ratings 48
Competitive Comparison 48
Verifying Your Data 51
Placement in the Quality House 52
The Doctor's Office 53
Exercise 55

Part II Technical Requirements (QFD)

Chapter 7 Technical Characteristics 59
Generating the Technical Requirements 61
Organizing the Technical Information 62
Customer Design Matrix Log 66
Developing the Quality House 69
The Doctor's Office 69
Exercises 77

Chapter 8 The Critical Relationships 79
Determination of Requirements 81
Determination of Relationships between Consequences and Requirements 81
Analyzing the Technical Matrix 86
Development of Measures 86
Setting Optimal Levels 87
Technical Competitive Analysis 88
The Doctor's Office 90
Exercises 93

Chapter 9 Technical Competitive Analysis 95
Customer Competitive Assessment 96
Technical Competitive Analysis 97
Comparing the Competitive Analyses 99
Marketing and Sales Analysis 101
The Doctor's Office 101
Exercises 105

Chapter 10 Technical Correlations and Trade-offs 107
Technical Correlations for the Roof of the Quality House . . 108
The Doctor's Office 113
Exercises 114

Chapter 11 Other Items to Consider in the Quality House . . . 115
Customer Complaint Column 116
Priority Column 117
Direction of Improvement 119
The Sales Improvement Column 122
Relative Importance of Technical Requirements 125
Customer Matrix 128
The Doctor's Office 128
Exercises 130

Chapter 12 Matrices for Parts, Processes, and Supplier Needs 131
Process Specifications 133
Parts Parameters 134
The Doctor's Office 135
Exercises 137

Part III Strategic Applications

Chapter 13 Using Your Results for Strategic Decisions 141
Prioritizing Resource Allocations 142
Value to the Customer 144
Market Segmentation 147
Brand Positioning 148
The Doctor's Office 150
Exercise 152

Chapter 14 An Example: A Laundry and Dry Cleaning Service 155
Voice of the Customer 156
Importance and Competitive Analysis 156
Technical Requirements 160
Developing Service Processes 163
Selecting Marketing Priorities and Strategies 165

Chapter 15 Making the Business Case 169
Cost Savings 170
Cycle-Time Reduction 171
Customer Satisfaction, Retention, and Loyalty 171

Lifetime Value of a Customer 173
Increased Sales 174
Greater Profits 174
Strategic Competitive Advantage 175

Chapter 16 Conclusions 177

Appendix A Cause-and-Effect (Fishbone) Diagram 181

Appendix B Designed Experiments 183

Appendix C Tree Diagram 185

Appendix D Benchmarking 187

Appendix E Block Diagrams 189

Appendix F The Malcolm Baldrige National Quality Award Process 191

Appendix G ANSI/ISO/ASQ Q9001-2000 and ISO/TS 16949 193

Appendix H The Six Sigma Process 195

Appendix I Answers to Chapter Exercises 197

Additional References 209

Index 211

List of Figures and Tables

Figure 1.1	The quality lever.	2
Table 1.1	ACSI ratings by industry.	3
Table 3.1	Attributes versus consequences.	19
Table 3.2	Attributes and consequences for some services.	19
Table 3.3	Attribute/consequence grid for a package delivery service.	20
Table 3.4a	Importance ratings for a package delivery service.	21
Table 3.4b	Brand ratings for a package delivery service.	21
Table 3.4c	Full compensatory model of decision making for a package delivery service.	22
Table 3.5	Attributes and consequences for appointment scheduling.	23
Table 3.6	Attribute/consequence grid for making appointments.	23
Table 3.7	Full compensatory model of decision making for a package delivery service.	24
Figure 4.1	Performance consequences.	29
Figure 4.2	Basic consequences.	29
Figure 4.3	Excitement consequences.	30
Figure 4.4	Sorted consequences for delivery services.	33
Figure 4.5	Grid for delivery service.	34
Figure 4.6	Grid for doctor's office.	35
Table 5.1	Brand ratings for pizza delivery.	38
Table 5.2	Weighted brand ratings for pizza delivery.	39
Figure 5.1	Rank order scale.	42
Figure 5.2	Itemized rating scale.	42
Figure 5.3	Constant sum scale.	43
Figure 5.4	Anchored scale.	44
Table 5.3	Comparison of scales.	44
Figure 5.5	Questionnaire for doctor's office.	45
Table 5.4	Mean rating for each consequence.	45
Figure 6.1	Competitive rating questionnaire for pizza delivery.	49
Table 6.1	Brand ratings for pizza delivery.	50
Table 6.2	Competitive profile for pizza delivery.	50
Table 6.3	Weighted brand ratings for pizza delivery.	51
Table 6.4	Customer section of the quality house.	52
Figure 6.2	Questionnaire for doctor's office.	53
Table 6.5	Weighted brand ratings for doctor's office.	54

Table 6.6	Competitive profile for the doctor's office.	55
Figure 7.1	Example of the process to this point.	60
Figure 7.2	Provide one or more hows for each what.	62
Figure 7.3	Three-layer tree diagram.	63
Figure 7.4	The pizza house delivery service needs example.	65
Figure 7.5	The tree diagram for developing technical ideas for a hot pizza.	65
Figure 7.6	An example of a tree diagram for delivery of a package.	66
Figure 7.7	Customer design matrix with measuring units and value of the measure for fulfilling customer needs.	67
Figure 7.8	Cause-and-effect diagram—the six Ms.	67
Figure 7.9	Cause-and-effect diagram for weather effects.	68
Figure 7.10	Cause-and-effect diagram for the fast delivery of pizza.	68
Figure 7.11	Cause-and-effect diagram for the delivery of hot pizza.	68
Figure 7.12	Quality house matrix with customer input and importance weightings.	71
Figure 7.13	Results of brainstorming technical concepts.	72
Figure 7.14	The tree diagram example for the doctor's office.	73
Figure 7.15	The doctor's office customer design matrix log.	73
Figure 7.16	The cause-and-effect diagram for doctors' appointments.	74
Figure 7.17	Beginning of the quality house.	74
Figure 7.18	The doctor's office example of customer needs to technical hows.	75
Figure 7.19	Quality house with customer input and requirements on the doctor's office call.	76
Figure 8.1	Flow of the concepts for this chapter.	80
Figure 8.2	Flow of steps.	81
Figure 8.3	The quality house with the customer's weighted input.	82
Figure 8.4	Customer design matrix log.	82
Figure 8.5	The quality house for pizza delivery with technical requirements.	83
Figure 8.6	Some hows affect more than one what.	84
Figure 8.7	Untangling the web.	84
Figure 8.8	The quality house for delivered pizza with relationships.	85
Figure 8.9	The delivery process with technical requirements for cost of delivery.	86
Figure 8.10	Examples of requirements with optimal values added.	87
Figure 8.11	The shipping process example of the completed matrix.	88
Figure 8.12	The quality house for delivered pizza with measures, directions, and values.	89
Figure 8.13	Process flowchart for doctor's office call.	90

Figure 8.14 Technical information matrix for making an appointment at the doctor's office. 90
Figure 8.15 The doctor's office example of relationships between customer consequences and technical requirements. 91
Figure 8.16 Example of the doctor's office correlation with the measures selected. 91
Figure 8.17 The doctor's office call with the matrix completed with requirements, measures, and relationships. 92
Figure 9.1 Competitive analysis for a delivery process. 98
Figure 9.2 Technical requirements for the customer needs of the delivered package. 100
Figure 9.3 Customer needs and technical requirements for a good tasting pizza. 100
Figure 9.4 The pizza quality house. 102
Figure 9.5 Doctor's office process specifications example. 103
Figure 9.6 Matrix of customer and technical evaluation comparisons. 104
Figure 10.1 A portion of the finished pizza quality house. 110
Figure 10.2 Matrix development for shipping. 111
Figure 10.3 A portion of the shipping process quality house. 112
Figure 10.4 A portion of the finished doctor's office quality house. 113
Figure 11.1 Pizza delivery process example with complaint column. 117
Figure 11.2 Pizza example with complaints, improvement goals, and priorities. 118
Figure 11.3 Cause-and-effect method for pizza toppings. 120
Figure 11.4 Cause-and-effect method for pizza toppings. 121
Figure 11.5 Cause-and-effect method for crispy crust. 121
Figure 11.6 Pizza technical specifications construction. 122
Figure 11.7 Pugh concept example. 124
Figure 11.8 Concept block diagram for the preparation, baking, and delivery processes for pizza. 125
Figure 11.9 Example of the concepts for the design of shipping processes. 125
Figure 11.10 Finished pizza house. 126
Figure 11.11 Made-up hotel room example. 127
Figure 11.12 Product service example for washing machine complaint. 128
Figure 11.13 Example matrix to match objectives to the customers. 129
Figure 11.14 The doctor's office example with complaints. 129
Figure 12.1 The four phases of quality function deployment. 132
Figure 12.2 Process parameter development for baking a pizza. 134
Figure 12.3 Part parameter development for preparing a pizza. 134
Figure 12.4 Shipping process example. 135
Figure 12.5 The doctor's office process parameters. 136
Figure 12.6 Doctor's office technical requirements. 137
Figure 13.1 Competitive profile for pizza delivery. 142
Table 13.1 Brand rating for pizza delivery. 143

Figure 13.2	Importance–performance grid for brand A pizza delivery.	144
Table 13.2	Weighted sums by brand for performance and price consequences.	145
Figure 13.3	Customer value map for pizza delivery.	146
Table 13.3	A portion of the importance ratings for pizza delivery.	147
Figure 13.4	Segmentation map for pizza delivery.	149
Figure 13.5	Alternative pizza delivery segmentation map.	149
Figure 13.6	Positioning map for pizza delivery.	150
Figure 13.7	Competitive profile for the doctor's office.	151
Figure 13.8	Importance–performance grid for the doctor's office.	151
Figure 13.9	Customer value map for doctor's office.	152
Table 14.1	Consequences for a laundry and dry cleaners.	157
Table 14.2	Questionnaire results.	158
Figure 14.1	Competitive grid.	159
Table 14.3	Technical requirements.	161
Figure 14.2	Relationship matrix.	162
Figure 14.3	Competitive technical assessment.	163
Table 14.4	Priority technical requirements.	164
Figure 14.4	Requirement correlations.	164
Figure 14.5	Completed house of quality.	165
Figure 14.6	The importance–performance grid.	166
Figure 14.7	Customer value map.	166
Table 15.1	Calculation of potential savings from customer retention.	173

Preface

This book provides you with a new approach that you can use to develop services that will exceed customers' expectations, maximize value, and build customer loyalty. Each chapter provides real-world examples, exercises, figures illustrating the processes, and references for further reading. Using the processes described in this book, you will develop stronger, more competitive service processes, gain competitive advantage in the marketplace, and grow your sales and market share.

ISO 9001:2000, the Malcolm Baldrige National Quality Award, and the Six Sigma approach to continuous improvement of processes all require that we understand customer needs and develop our products and services to achieve customer satisfaction. Despite this continuing emphasis on customers, many organizations still do not systematically incorporate the voice of their customers into their operations.

The authors have repeatedly observed this failure to effectively use the customers' voice during their long careers as professional engineer and marketer, Malcolm Baldrige examiners, college professors, and consultants. This book is the product of their years of teaching and consulting to industry on the need to establish a means to understand the needs of the market and individual customers. The authors address the methods for obtaining customer needs for service industries and for translating these needs into requirements for services. We also provide examples targeted to service industries and the service side of manufacturing.

Despite numerous books on customer research and many other books on quality function deployment, none has effectively integrated the two areas to create a total process for spreading the needs and wants of the customer throughout the operations of the company. Over the years of teaching together in the Master of Quality Management program at Loyola University New Orleans, the authors have developed a process that combines these two fields together. The result is a method that effectively integrates the voice of the customer into product and service development and uses these results to guide strategic planning for the organization.

The authors have taught this method to over 100 students and guided its use in nearly as many applied projects for organizations. Its effectiveness is shown both subjectively and by actual bottom-line results. The organizations using this approach have become much more competitive, even in today's global marketplace. The results are remarkably greater sales and greater profits.

This book is a practical guide for the development of the voice of the customer and quality function deployment, which when used as outlined will allow the service organization to focus on the needs of the various customers together. The process is not a simple one; it takes extensive teamwork within the organization. The authors have found that the application of this process is more difficult for services, probably because customer needs for services are highly perceptual and harder to measure. The lack of written examples for services also impedes implementation in this area. However, the process does work very well for service organizations and for the services provided by manufacturing organizations when these organizations understand and apply it in the service context.

Prior books on quality function deployment have focused on manufacturing. Translation to the service arena has been difficult for most people. The authors decided to focus this book on services to assist understanding of how these techniques apply in a service setting. The examples used in the book are service oriented. They come from student projects conducted for their organizations and from the authors' consulting experiences.

The unique features of this book are the process and methods of securing information that will develop customer benefits from needs and wants. The process also covers how to distinguish between the needs and wants as consequences and attributes of the customer and ranking them for further processing of the information. We use the proven tools to establish the technical ways to achieve customer satisfaction against the needs and wants.

This book contains material that aids in understanding the process of obtaining the customer's voice and linking it to the design process, which will provide the technical process features to deliver the customers' needs from the process output. The sequence of steps helps provide increased customer satisfaction, increased market share, a reduced number of non-value-added processes, and a more effective approach for marketing the service. If your organization is in the process of pursuing the Six Sigma approach, you should begin the process with learning how to obtain the customer voice and developing the technical requirements that will help you in meeting these needs. Design and process engineers will find that the approaches used will benefit them in their search to obtain the true customer needs and expectations. Readers can use this book as a text for teaching the principles of voice of the customer and quality function deployment to students in management or engineering programs.

Chapter 1

Introduction

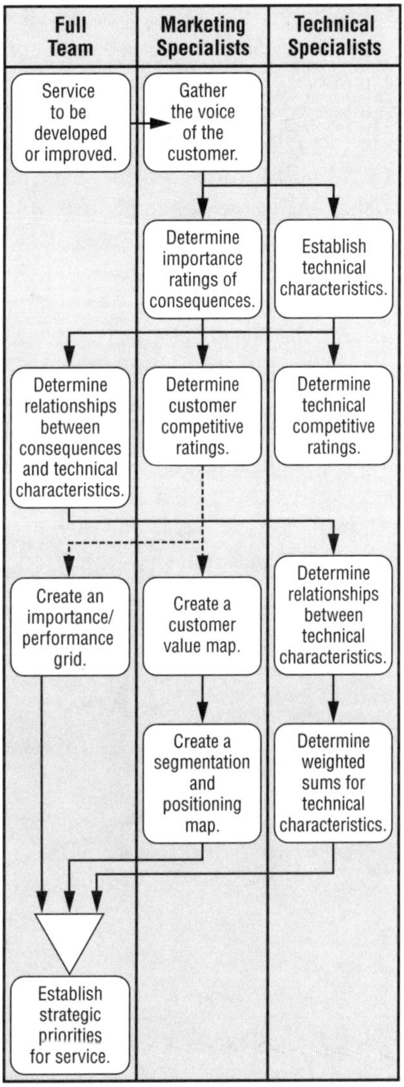

CHAPTER TOPICS

- Quality Function Deployment
- Services
- QFD for Services

Quality function deployment (QFD) is a system for translating consumer requirements into appropriate company requirements at each stage, from research and product development to engineering and manufacturing to marketing/sales and distribution. QFD has a long history of use in manufacturing since its development by Shigeru Mizuno, Yoji Akao, and others in Japan more than 30 years ago.[1]

QFD has many advantages over traditional product and process development processes. When using QFD, companies find that they make fewer changes during the development process, and those that they do make occur earlier during the process when making them is less expensive. The problems and required changes that occur at the introduction of the new product or service and in the field are far fewer. These fewer and earlier changes result in shorter development times, lower development costs, and greater profits, as illustrated by the quality lever in Figure 1.1. QFD moves quality control upstream from manufacturing to product design. Efforts to assure quality during the design phase have 100 times the impact of similar efforts during the manufacturing phase.

Other advantages of using QFD are harder for us to quantify, but may provide even greater benefits to the organization. During the QFD process, the organization develops a proprietary knowledge base about its customers and their needs and wants. Not only does this knowledge base help the organization develop products and services that satisfy customers and increase sales in the short term, it also helps the organization anticipate future customer desires. This enhanced ability to predict future customer needs gives the organization a marketing advantage that is difficult for competitors to duplicate and therefore is long-term in its impact.

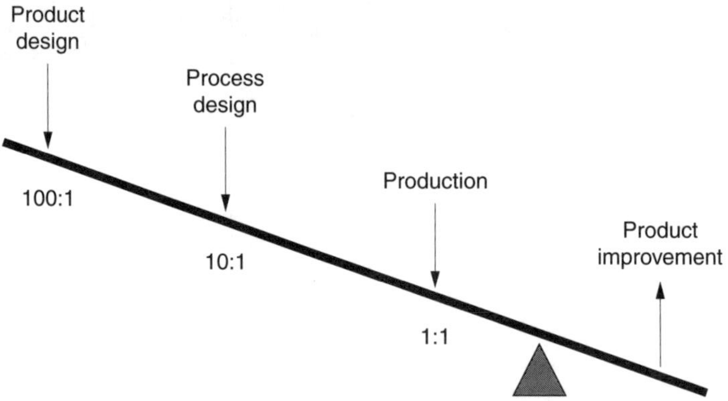

Figure 1.1 The quality lever.

SERVICES

Service organizations make up a significant and growing portion of the United States and world economy. It is estimated that private-sector services made up two-thirds of the gross domestic product of the United States in 2001. The service sector has increased significantly in the last decade, with high-technology services projected to grow by 25 percent during the next three to five years.[2] Service industries such as banking, hotels, restaurants, travel, healthcare, education, and many more play critical roles in our economy.

Customer satisfaction for service industries is lower than that of manufacturing industries, with the lone exceptions of personal computers and parcel delivery, as measured by the American Customer Satisfaction Index (ACSI).[3] Begun in 1994 by the University of Michigan Business School, the American Society for Quality, and the CFI Group, the ACSI tracks customer satisfaction quarterly for a variety of industries. Table 1.1 shows the most recent ACSI scores by industry. The ACSI is highly important because

Table 1.1 ACSI ratings by industry.

Industry	Time Period	ACSI
Overall	Q2 2002	73
Manufacturing Durables	Q2 2002	79
Personal computers	Q2 2002	71
Household appliances	Q2 2002	82
Consumer electronics	Q2 2002	81
Automobiles	Q2 2002	80
Manufacturing Nondurables	Q3 2001	80
Food processing	Q3 2001	82
Services		
Financial	Q4 2001	76
Retail	Q4 2001	75
E-business	Q2 2002	69
Healthcare	Q1 2002	68
Airlines	Q1 2002	66
Telecommunications	Q1 2002	71
Parcel delivery	Q1 2002	79
TV	Q1 2002	61
Utilities	Q1 2002	73
Hotels	Q1 2002	71

Source: www.theacsi.org/industry_scores.htm

it correlates with the gross domestic product, personal spending, the stock market, and stock prices of individual firms.[4]

Service industries have been slower to adopt total quality management, ISO 9000, the Baldrige standards, and other approaches to increasing quality. Even when an organization adopts these approaches, the absence of defects does not guarantee customer satisfaction. QFD is one approach that directly addresses customer needs and wants, and affects customer satisfaction significantly. These service industries could greatly benefit from the use of QFD.

INTERNAL SERVICES

Internal service providers abound in every organization. Accounting, personnel, information management, purchasing, and other internal service groups are vital to the success of the organization. When manufacturing organizations apply QFD, they generally apply it to product development for external customers.

QFD FOR SERVICES

Most books about QFD largely ignore the service industry. Most, if not all, examples used in such books relate to manufacturing organizations and product development processes. However, some service organizations have applied QFD for many years. Early applications of QFD to services in Japan included a shopping mall, a sports complex, and retail stores.[5] Florida Power and Light used QFD as part of its efforts that won it the Japanese Deming Prize in 1990.[6] The University of Michigan Medical Center used QFD as early as 1991.[7] Some higher education institutions have used QFD in developing curriculum and programs.[8]

Both manufacturing and service organizations have applied QFD to internal service systems. One example was the application of QFD at a university research resource center at Tennessee Technological University's College of Business Administration.[9] The authors worked with an internal purchasing department at a corporate 100 company to help it design purchasing services that provided value to its internal customers. In this organization, use of the internal purchasing services was not required; the department changed its services to increase usage rates.

THE PURPOSE OF THIS BOOK

The purpose of this book is to explain, by example, the various ways of obtaining customers' service needs and expectations. From the proper prioritization of those needs, we then show how we align the customers' needs to the requirements that we have to deliver within the process. Many different examples show how organizations use the various tools to point the organization in the right direction. Many organizations are now applying Six Sigma tools to improve their customer performance. The voice of the customer and quality function deployment are part of the tool base that is used in the Six Sigma process. Most training does not provide all the different methods or approaches that one can use to develop the customers' voice and the requirement internally to meet those needs from the voice of the customer. Our book provides you with the methods that assist with the most critical part of the Six Sigma process. If we do not start with clean, realistic data, we may develop a process that meets the wrong needs or misses needs of our customers. This book closes the gap that exists within the Six Sigma training programs. With the approaches we show, you will be even more successful in your Six Sigma program.

Part I of this book focuses on the voice of the customer. The first four chapters cover how to interview and survey customers to understand the set of consequences that they are trying to resolve with the service that you provide. If the organization follows this approach, it will identify needs in the customers' terms. We then need to prioritize the wants or needs and use this input to develop the approaches we use to satisfy those needs.

Part II focuses on the use of the quality house to develop the technical requirements of the process to meet those needs. The next five chapters cover the techniques used in both service and manufacturing industries to use the voice of the customer, as prioritized by the customer, to define the process requirements that are required to deliver the service. The customers need or expect organizations to provide this service. The design team needs to evaluate and define the concepts that exist for the process. This design process requires interpretation of the customers' voice and a check to verify that, indeed, we interpreted the voice properly. Defining process requirements requires several steps in the concept phase to evaluate the alternatives that exist to satisfy customers' needs. This process requires the use of the familiar tools of cause-and-effect diagrams, tree diagrams, and relationship diagrams. From the analysis, we determine which concepts help us meet the needs of the customer and the alternatives to use to meet them.

Once we have determined the design concepts, we need to indicate the measures we will use to verify that the requirements for the process will fulfill the customers' needs. We test these requirements against the needs of the customer. Once we agree on the requirements and the measurement level, then we proceed to evaluate the matrix that we developed between the customers' needs and the requirements. The final matrix evaluation will determine if we have met all the needs of the customer and if the requirements are still valid. From this matrix, we form different matrices to evaluate the process parameters that need to be in place and the means of control to assure that the process will be capable of delivering the requirements that the design team initially established.

Part III comes full circle by making the business case for QFD. It then provides a full project from a service organization as an example of using the procedures detailed in parts one and two. As you proceed through the various chapters, keep in mind the competitive edge obtainable by using the process we have developed in using the critical tools that start the Six Sigma or lean Six Sigma process.

The process described in the following chapters follows 12 distinct steps, which are:

1. Determine attributes desired by the customer.
2. Determine consequences tied to these attributes.
3. Rank customer consequences.
4. Conduct a customer competitive analysis.
5. Determine technical requirements to meet customers' needs.
6. Relate the voice of the customer to the technical requirements and the ability to deliver those requirements.
7. Determine measurement methods and goals for technical requirements.
8. Complete a technical analysis of performance compared to the competition.
9. Relate technical requirements to each other to identify potential conflicts.
10. Analyze regulatory requirements.
11. Weight the requirements to set priorities.
12. Develop competitive analyses and determine strategies.

These steps are easy when taken one at a time. If you perform the steps in sequence, your knowledge base about your market and customers will increase tenfold. Once you have gained market knowledge, you will know what it takes to become the market leader in your industry. Take on the challenge and try it.

ENDNOTES

1. Glenn H. Mazur, "QFD for Service Industries: From Voice of Customer to Task Deployment," The Fifth Symposium on Quality Function Deployment, Novi, MI, 1993.
2. Daniel Hays and John Riggs, "New Beginnings: Moving from Products to Services," *Marketing Management* (July/August 2002): 38–42.
3. The American Customer Satisfaction Index can be found at http://www.theacsi.org/ .
4. Claes Fornell, "Q2, 2002: Manufacturing Durables and E-Business," http://www.theacsi.org/scores_commentaries/commentaries , 2002.
5. Yoji Akao, ed., *Quality Function Deployment: Integrating Customer Requirements into Product Design*, trans. Glenn Mazur (Cambridge, MA: Productivity Press, 1990).
6. Joseph L. Webb and W. C. Hayes, "Quality Function Deployment at FPL," *Transactions from the Second Symposium on Quality Function Deployment*, Novi, MI, 1990.
7. Ellen Gaucher, T. Daly, J. Walker, and V. Walter, "Quality Function Deployment Process: Experiences in an Ambulatory Care Service," *Proceedings from the GOAL/QPC Eighth Annual Conference* (Boston, MA: GOAL/QC, 1991).
8. Caroline Fisher and Elizabeth Weymann, "Participative Curriculum Planning: Including Student and Company Voices," *Journal of Innovative Management* 4, no. 4 (1999): 34–44.
9. Nat Natarajan, Ralph E. Martz, and Kyosuke Kurosaka, "Applying QFD to Internal Service System Design," *Quality Progress* (February 1999): 65–70.

Chapter 2

Voice of the Customer and Quality Function Deployment Overview

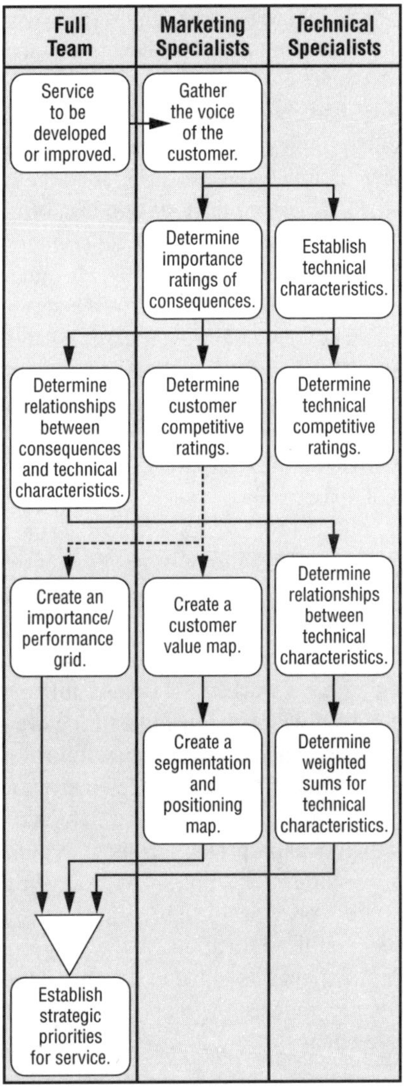

CHAPTER TOPICS

- The Overview of the Process
- The Customers' Voice
- The Quality House
- The Customers' Use of the Service

The quality systems of most large corporations and small companies require that the organization identify its customers and the marketplace that they are addressing. This is not a small task; we must perform it properly to assure that we are knowledgeable about the true customers, their needs, and the actual users of our service. We have found, through practice, that we need to focus on the identification of the market and the customers who will use the service that the organization provides to the market. Organizations usually do not identify their markets and customers because they think they know their customers' needs. Companies are still facing greater challenges than ever in meeting those customer needs and the increasing demands customers and employees are requiring in a changing socioeconomic and technological environment. The company is compelled to incorporate all efforts to continuously improve services to best satisfy their customers and at the same time to make a profit and enhance their competitiveness. The founder of quality function deployment, Yoji Akao, described the QFD portion of the process as a method for developing a design quality aimed at satisfying the customer and then translating the customers' demand into the design targets and major quality assurance points to be used throughout the service provision stage of the process.

The new quality standards, such as ISO 9001: 2000, ISO 16949:2000, and AS9100, require that organizations obtain and review customer satisfaction and dissatisfaction regularly and systematically. They also require that a process be in place to identify customers' needs. Specifically, ISO 16949 requires that we have a process in place to detect customers' needs and expectations and a process to develop those needs into technical requirements through an engineering process that develops internal specifications. This allows us to develop key characteristics that must be met and controlled to meet the needs of our customers.

The processes we use to develop service customers' needs and the key design and process characteristics required to meet the needs of the customer have worked for several different service organizations and services provided within the manufacturing organization. The quality function deployment tool helps the organization move toward a more proactive process development for the service environment. QFD becomes a customer-driven quality management system, which incorporates the voice of the customer into the appropriate technical requirements at each stage in the design process through implementation of the process and its controls. The QFD process provides designed-in quality rather than inspected-in quality. The successful application of the voice of the customer and quality function deployment has reduced development time for processes, lowered start-up costs, promoted the use of teams, and reduced after-the-introduction reactive changes.

Chapters 3 through 6 take you through the steps in the development of the customers' voice. The customers that we address and the market that we are in are first determined. From this starting point, we then develop methods that allow us to interview, test, and exchange ideas that cover the consequences of the customer. This begins with a review of consumer choice decisions in chapter 3. The consequences developed in chapter 4 lead us to the attributes required to fulfill the needs of the customer. The interview process provides the details that cover how customers are meeting their needs today and how satisfied they are with the results. We also uncover needs that are unfulfilled today, leading us to develop a service process that will satisfy those missed needs. This is the most important part of the entire process. If we do not understand the customers' consequences or the attributes they require, we will have flaws in the rest of the development and delivery process to the customer. Studying chapters 3 and 4 shows how the process of customer and consequence identification is accomplished. In chapter 4, we develop the process for identification of the consequences from the attributes. We must perform this identification with care so we provide the correct consequences to the development team that transposes the consequences into technical characteristics.

Chapter 5 takes us through the ranking or ordering of the developed needs and expectations of the customer. The data and information provided by this process help us transform the customers' needs to the internal technical requirements of the processes that deliver our service to our customers. Realize that the needs of customers may vary depending on the market or customer base that we address. This sometimes requires us to reconsider which customers we address and the process or processes that are required to meet their different or varying needs. Chapter 5 helps us create the importance rating of the attributes developed from the customers' input. This may require a second visit to the customer group after the attributes are determined. Usually, we cannot prioritize the list of attributes during focus groups or interviews with customers because these customers do not adequately represent the customer group; we have not randomly selected them from the total population of customers. In situations where we have a limited number of customers and interview all of them, we sometimes prioritize the attributes as we identify them.

In chapter 6, we capture the competitive analysis of the service from the viewpoint of the same customer group that established the importance of the consequences. Often we complete this competitive rating at the same time we investigate the importance of the consequences, with one questionnaire. This competitive analysis needs to show how well each particular need is being fulfilled today both by us and by our competitors. The rating usually uses a one-to-five point scale. A good question list using the previously identified consequences obtains good relative ratings. This comparative evaluation may use our direct competition, or it may evaluate the way consumers are attempting to meet their desired consequences today.

We must complete this customer input process for the QFD process to be effective in developing a service process that meets or exceeds customers' needs. We use the customers' desired consequences and their weightings as the input or left side of the quality matrix, as explained in chapter 7. This chapter starts with the process of developing technical requirements and progresses through an analysis of the correlation of the matrix of the customer needs and the technical requirements. The critical analysis of the matrix is then reviewed and analyzed in chapter 8.

Once we know our market and our customers, we use the quality house to develop technical requirements and check various aspects of the process that we must review to exceed customers' wants and needs. The matrix of the quality house is the analysis process that keeps the voice of the customer tied to the technical requirements developed in chapter 7 and establishes the critical relationships between customers' needs and the technical requirements for the technical personnel. The technical personnel involved with the development of the requirements for the process or product are discussed in chapter 8. We may use one of several methods to develop the technical requirements for the process or product. These methods vary based on the organization and the service we are providing. This section of the quality house is very important and requires a cross-functional team that determines the process steps required to meet the needs of the customer and the measures required to control the processes that provide output to the customers. When we establish the customers' needs for the input to the house, we are very careful to assure we are addressing the various customers to whom we sell our services. The technical evaluation requires that the proper disciplines of the organization are present to assure that they develop the process properly to meet those needs. The technical personnel must be present for process development.

Once we have the technical process developed, then we need to evaluate the matrix using the same personnel. The evaluation of the matrix is covered in chapter 8 and followed up in chapters 9 and 10. Chapter 9 describes the technical competitive analysis at the bottom of the matrix. In chapter 10, we cover the correlations and trade-offs in the design process by evaluating the roof of the house. The same technical team specifies these correlations. When we have completed this portion of the matrix, we are now ready to look at other ways to evaluate customers' needs and technical requirements with other columns of information.

The quality house is a valuable screening tool that ties customers' requirements to the organization's strengths and areas for improvement using numerical values obtained during the matrix analysis process. We must take care when using the numerical values that we do not misinterpret them or use them outside the context of their development. We may use them to highlight customers' desires and the organization's strengths in meeting those needs against the competition and note our capabilities to meet these needs. The mathematics used in the analysis of these data is covered in chapters 9 and 10. Chapter 11 discusses additional information that is developed from the house of quality. Once we have this room of the house completed, we consider other rooms. Chapter 12 takes us through the use of the output from the first room to develop the needs for the process, supplier requirements, and process controls. The chapter addresses how to develop the other requirements from the input to the right side of the room, using the same concepts we used for the first room of the house. Chapter 12 also addresses the entire house with the relationships for a final analysis. This establishes the needs for the next room of the house that we prioritize by the relationships that we developed from the matrix analysis for the customer wants and the developed requirements.

Two dominant models exist for the quality house: the four-phase or room model, sometimes called the Clausing model or the ASI model; and Akao's model of matrix of matrices. The four-phase model divides the development process into four phases or steps using four different rooms or matrices. The first phase collects the customers' needs for the service, called *wants,* and then transforms these needs into technical measures for the organization, called *hows.* The quality house then links the customer needs to the technical responses that meet the needs. The second phase transforms the prioritized technical measures in the first phase to process requirements. We then transform the key process requirements into the key process characteristics that we must control to deliver the requirements in phase three. The last phase establishes the key process controls to ensure meeting the specified requirements.

Once we have a complete house of quality matrix, then we conduct further analyses to assist us with strategic decision making. In chapter 13, we develop a competitive profile, an importance–performance matrix, a customer value map, and a segmentation and positioning map. These strategic tools help us identify where to work to improve our processes to have the greatest impact on customer value and customers' purchasing decisions. Finally, chapter 14 shows us how to make the business case, using bottom-line analyses, to proceed with our improvements.

Part I

Voice of the Customer

Chapter 3

Understanding Consumer Choice Decisions

CHAPTER TOPICS

- Attributes and Consequences
- Compensatory Decision-Making Model

CHAPTER TOOLS

- Attribute/Consequence Grid
- Predicting Compensatory Decision Making

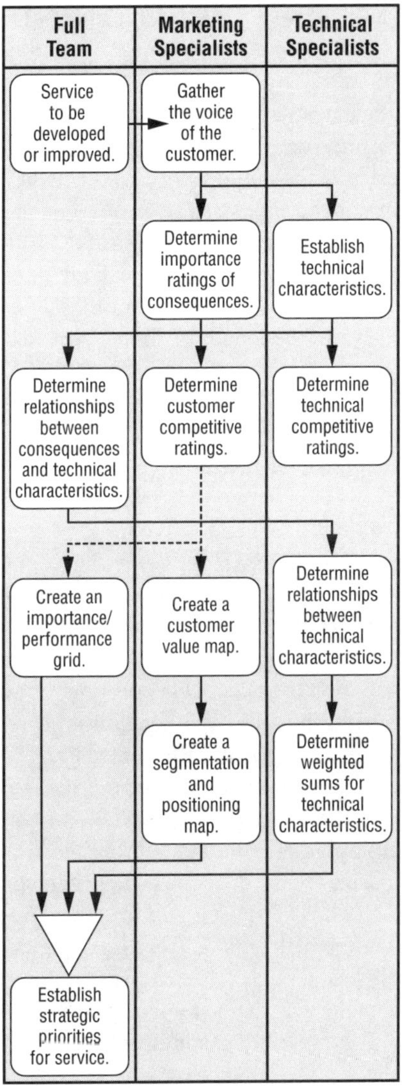

As service providers, we are interested in getting people to choose our services and pay for them. In order to get people to choose our services, we need to understand how they select which service they will use. How do consumers select our service out of all those that are available? Research has shown that consumers select services that provide consequences that they value. They do not buy based on attributes. What is the difference between an attribute and consequence?

ATTRIBUTES AND CONSEQUENCES

As service providers, we tend to think of our services in terms of their attributes or features. But consumers are not so much interested in service features or attributes or even the services themselves. They are really interested in the consequences of using our services. Customers buy services for their benefits or positive consequences, not their attributes.

Attributes are the physical or abstract characteristics of the service. Consequences, on the other hand, are the results of using the service. Attributes are generally objective and measurable. For example, we can objectively measure the length of time a person stands in line (attribute: short waiting times) using a stopwatch. On the other hand, not having to wait a long time is subjective, and we cannot measure it except through the perception of the person waiting. Indeed, what seems like a short wait on one occasion may seem like an interminable wait on another, even to the same person, because of different reasons for waiting or different conflicting time requirements leading to a need to save time.

As this example points out, consequences are subjective; they are in the eye of the consumer and are very individual. Consequences include customer perceptions of convenience. A consumer values an attribute only because of its perceived capacity to create a desired consequence through use of the service. One consumer may perceive one consequence for using a service, while another consumer may perceive a very different consequence from using the same service. Consequences exist only if the user perceives them. Consequences are strictly from the viewpoint of the user, not from the viewpoint of the service provider who may have a very different opinion about the appropriateness of the waiting time.[1] Table 3.1 summarizes these differences between consequences and attributes.

The U.S. Postal Service is the biggest letter-delivery service in terms of volume of letters delivered. People do not use its services because it is the biggest, though. They may use it, for example, because it can deliver a letter anywhere; it can get a letter to the smallest town in the United States. Table 3.2 shows other examples of services and their attributes and consequences.

Table 3.1 Attributes versus consequences.

Attributes	Consequences
Attributes are physical or abstract characteristics of the service.	Consequences are a result of using the service.
Attributes are objective.	Consequences are subjective.
Attributes are measurable.	Consequences are measured through surveys of users' perceptions.
Attributes are from the producer's viewpoint.	Consequences are from the consumer's viewpoint.

Table 3.2 Attributes and consequences for some services.

Service	Attribute	Consequence
Printing	Accuracy	I get what I need.
Delivery	Fast	I get my materials quickly.
Office cleaning	Effective	My office is clean.
Purchasing	Best price	I stay within budget.

A service usually has many attributes. For example, an internal purchasing department may have quick turnaround, offer the best prices, require few steps in ordering, and provide in-depth knowledge about the product you want to order. The quick turnaround may help you get a product quickly in an emergency. The best price may mean you can stay within budget. The few ordering steps may make ordering convenient and hassle-free. The in-depth knowledge about the product you want to order may assist in getting the product that will best meet your requirements.

In addition to services having more than one attribute, one attribute may lead to more than one consequence. For example, an efficient office cleaning service may provide not only a clean office, but also get in the way of employees less and keep the number of ants in the kitchen area down.

Because of the number of attributes and consequences and their many relationships, we often use an attribute/consequence grid to visually display the relationships. Table 3.3 shows an attribute/consequence grid for a package delivery service. The attributes are in the first column, and the consequences are in the first row. When a positive relationship exists between a consequence and an attribute, we place a "+" in the cell where the two intersect. When a negative relationship exists, we place a "–" in that cell. The number of pluses or minuses indicates the strength of the relationship. If no relationship exists, we leave the cell blank. In Table 3.3, depicting an attribute/consequence grid for a package delivery service, we

Table 3.3 Attribute/consequence grid for a package delivery service.

	Consequences			
Attributes	**Overnight**	**Delivered the day I want**	**No damage**	**Within budget**
Speedy	+++	+		–
Exact time	+	+++		–
Careful			+++	–
Low cost	–	–	–	+++
Accurate				–

see a strong positive relationship between careful and no damage; we see a negative relationship between careful and within budget.

Normally, a team including people who are intimately familiar with the customers and those who are intimately familiar with the product or service completes this grid. The former may be people from marketing, front line customer service, or those who interviewed the customers. The latter are usually people from operations. This combination helps assure that we indicate all important relationships, but do not mark insignificant relationships. Likewise, we want to avoid marking relationships that may occur because of how we operate, but that are not absolute rules. An example of this from Table 3.3 would be the relationship between speedy and no damage. While such a relationship might occur if speed of delivery led to lack of attention to care, that relationship could and should be avoided by designing our processes well.

So, now we know that consumers select services based on the consequences they expect to receive. However, we still do not know how they select one brand of service out of the many available. Consumers select the service provider that offers the greatest value overall, when all the consumers' needs and wants are considered. The compensatory decision-making model illustrates how this decision is made.

COMPENSATORY DECISION-MAKING MODEL

Compensatory decision making is a highly logical process that involves rating competing service brands on relevant criteria, weighting them by an importance factor, and then summing these weighted ratings. The consumer selects the brand with the highest sum. For a specific brand, strength on one criterion can compensate for a weakness on another criterion, leading to the compensatory term in the title of the model.

Let us look at an example for three hypothetical brands of delivery services. We call the delivery companies or brands Acme, Bell, and Class. First, we need the list of important consequences for using delivery services listed in Table 3.3. Then we add the consumer's ratings of the importance of each of these consequences (see Table 3.4a). Let us say that our consumer rates them as follows on a scale of zero to 10, zero being the least important and 10 being the most important. We discuss how to get these importance ratings in chapter 5.

Next, we add the consumer's ratings of each brand on each consequence. Again, we use a 10-point scale. The ratings for each brand are under the brand name (see Table 3.4b). For example, Bell was rated a six on "Delivered the day I want." We discuss how to get these brand ratings in chapter 6.

Now we use the model to calculate the brand of delivery service that this particular consumer will select. The brand rating on a consequence multiplied by the importance rating of that consequence gives a weighted rating, one where we weight the brand rating by the importance. We repeat this calculation for each brand on each consequence. Then we sum these weighted ratings for each of the service brands. These sums are in the bottom row (see Table 3.4c).

Table 3.4a Importance ratings for a package delivery service.

Consequence	Importance Rating
Delivered overnight	5
Delivered the day I want	10
No damage	9
Within budget	10

Table 3.4b Brand ratings for a package delivery service.

Consequences	Importance Rating	Brand Rating		
		Acme	Bell	Class
Delivered overnight	5	10	2	7
Delivered the day I want	10	4	6	4
No damage	9	10	8	4
Within budget	10	5	8	10

Table 3.4c Full compensatory model of decision making for a package delivery service.

Consequences	Importance Rating	Acme		Bell		Class	
		Rating	Weighted Rating	Rating	Weighted Rating	Rating	Weighted Rating
Delivered overnight	5	10	50	2	10	7	35
Delivered the day I want	10	4	40	6	60	4	40
No damage	9	10	90	8	72	4	36
Within budget	10	5	50	8	80	10	100
Sum of weighted ratings			230		222		211

The calculations show us that this consumer would choose the Acme brand despite its low rating on "Delivered the day I want." Its strength on other consequences, especially on "no damage," more than compensates for that weakness.

The emphasis on "this consumer" is critical. As stated in the attributes and consequences section, consequences are subjective and very individual. We cannot assume that two consumers will want the same consequences, nor that they will rate the importance of a consequence or the brand ratings on that consequence the same, even when they do want the same consequence. We have to make these measurements and calculations for each individual in order to predict purchase behavior. We talk about measuring importance in chapter 5 and brand ratings in chapter 6.

Another method we use when we have a large number of consumers is to divide them into groups or segments based on their ratings of the importance of a list of consequences. We want to determine consumer segments that desire very similar consequences, and we want each segment to be as different from the other segments as possible on desired consequences. Fortunately, statistical software determines these segments for us using techniques such as cluster analysis. Once we determine the consumer segments, then we determine averages for each segment on importance ratings, brand ratings, and sums of weighted ratings for each brand. Then we predict purchase choice fairly well for each segment.

We return to the topic of segmentation in chapter 12. Next, we want to look at how we actually learn which consequences are important to consumers so we can construct the tables shown in this chapter.

THE DOCTOR'S OFFICE

The staff of a doctor's office used probing techniques to interview 30 of the doctor's patients about the office's appointment system. They found that most of the patients mentioned the same items, but they continued to provide some new items throughout the interviews. The staff developed the list of items shown in Table 3.5 from the results of the interviews.

Next, the staff developed the attribute/consequence grid in Table 3.6 from the results of the interviews.

Table 3.5 Attributes and consequences for appointment scheduling.

Attributes	Consequences
Length of time until appointment	I got an appointment within a week of my call
Rings until call was answered	I had my choice of days
Time on hold	I had my choice of times
I was passed from person to person	I spent little time on the phone
I was asked few needless questions	I was treated courteously
Use of automated phone system	I was not put on hold

Table 3.6 Attribute/consequence grid for making appointments.

	Consequences				
Attributes	I got an appointment within a week of my call	I was not put on hold	I was asked few needless questions	I had my choice of days and times	I spent little time on the phone
Length of time until appointment	+++			–	
Rings until call was answered					+++
Time on hold		– – –	–		– – –
Use of automated phone system		++			+
Number of contacts on path to appointment		– – –	– –		– – –
Number of questions asked		– –	– – –		– – –

Table 3.7 Full compensatory model of decision making for a package delivery service.

Consequences	Importance Rating	Acme		Bell		Class	
		Rating	Weighted Rating	Rating	Weighted Rating	Rating	Weighted Rating
Delivered overnight	10	10		2		7	
Delivered the day I want	10	4		6		4	
No damage	8	10		8		4	
Within budget	5	5		8		10	
Sum of weighted ratings							

EXERCISES

1. Separate the items below into lists of attributes and consequences for coffee houses. Develop an attribute/consequence grid showing the relationships between the attributes and the consequences.

Coffee tastes good	My friends go there
Pastries are offered	Competitive prices
Quiet atmosphere	Quick service
Tables available	Friendly service
I can get my coffee quickly	I can study there
Located near my home	I can socialize there
Many flavors of coffee offered	Computers available to rent

2. Determine which brand the consumer would select using the numbers provided in Table 3.7.

ENDNOTE

1. See Robert B. Woodruff and Sarah F. Gardial, *Know Your Customer: New Approaches to Understanding Customer Value and Satisfaction* (Cambridge, MA: Blackwell Publishers, 1996): 64–69 for further discussion of the differences between attributes and consequences.

Chapter 4

Voice of the Customer

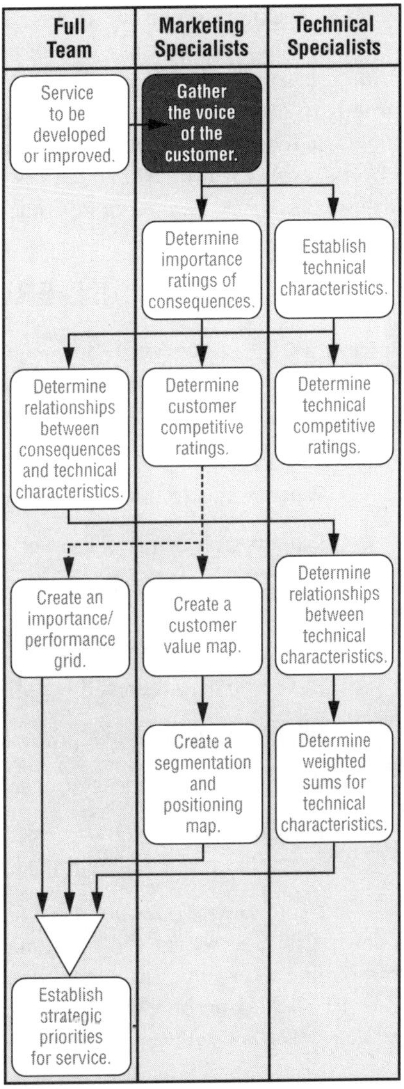

CHAPTER TOPICS

- Interviews
- Focus Groups
- The Modified Kano Model
- Identifying the Consequences from the Interview Transcripts
- Other Sources of Data
- Organizing the Customer Voice
- Finding and Adding Missing Consequences

CHAPTER TOOLS

- Depth Interviews
- Focus Groups
- Affinity Diagram
- Customer Sort
- Attribute/Consequence Grid

As stated in chapter 3, consequences are subjective; they are in the eye of the consumer and are very individualized. The only way to determine consequences is to ask the consumer, that is, to obtain the voice of the customer directly. Two primary ways to obtain the voice of the customer are through interviews or focus groups. In both cases, we ask the customer what is important to them in selecting our service. Most often, consumers give us service attributes, such as speedy service. Since we are looking for the consequences, as explained above, we ask "why" or probe for the underlying consequences tied to any attribute a customer gives in response to our questions.

We want to identify as many of the important consequences as we can, within reason. Research has shown that it takes 30 interviews or five focus groups to obtain 90 percent of customer consequences.[1] Additional interviews or focus groups yield additional consequences, but these additional efforts result in diminishing returns. In most situations, we are satisfied with obtaining 90 percent of customer consequences.

INTERVIEWS

Interviews are one-on-one conversations where the interviewer keeps the conversation focused. The interviewer leads the discussion through prepared questions to get the desired information. Typical questions used in interviews to obtain customer consequences for pizza delivery are:

- What comes to mind when you think of pizza delivery?
- What brands of pizza can you name?
- Which brand do you normally select?
- Why do you choose that brand?
- Have you ever received bad pizza delivery? Tell me about it.
- What would your ideal pizza delivery be like?
- What is important to you in selecting a pizza delivery service?
- Walk me through the process of deciding to order a pizza through eating the pizza and getting rid of the trash.

The interviewer does not use every question with each consumer. One question is used to get the consumer talking. When the consumer stops responding to one question, then the interviewer asks another question.

To elicit consequences from consumers, we use a technique called *probing*. The interviewer takes each attribute mentioned by the consumer and asks "why." We vary the wording of the question using some of the following forms:

- Why is that important to you?
- Why do you say that?
- What do you mean by that?
- Why do you want _____?
- What would happen if you didn't get _____?

Listening, probing, and writing down responses are too much for one person to do. We might use a second person to write down the responses, but usually we audiotape or videotape our interview sessions to make sure we capture everything the customer says. Someone transcribes these tapes later so others in the organization can read them, or a variety of people in the organization may each listen to them.

FOCUS GROUPS

We use focus groups to gain the same information that interviews do, but with a group of people at a time. The biggest advantage of a focus group is that the members of the group tend to stimulate ideas from each other, much like brainstorming. A trained moderator usually runs the focus groups because working with groups is more difficult than working with individuals. Someone who has training as a facilitator probably has the skills necessary to run a focus group for purposes of acquiring the voice of the customer.

Each focus group includes from seven to 12 consumers who are similar in demographics. The reason that we bring similar people together is that they tend to communicate with each other more readily than people who vary from each other significantly. In addition, the similarity in the consequences they desire helps them stimulate additional ideas from other members of the group.

The moderator of the focus group develops a series of questions in preparation for running the session. The questions are the same as those asked in interviews; the main difference is that we give all participants an opportunity to answer each question. Again, the moderator asks one question, then gives all the participants an opportunity to answer it fully. We use probing in much the same way in the focus group as in the individual interviews. When the group has finished answering the question and its probes, then the moderator asks another question.

Like the interviewer, the moderator cannot conduct the group, listen and probe, and write down the responses. Using a second person to write down responses is more common during focus group sessions. The sessions may be audio taped, but more often, we videotape them. We also use special rooms with one-way mirrors for some focus groups; people who have a stake in hearing what the consumers have to say may listen and watch from the other side of the mirror.

One of the biggest challenges in using focus groups is getting these groups of people together at the same time and place. Often, we must pay the participants to get them to come. The cost varies dramatically with the type of person being included in a focus group. Professionals tend to be more expensive because of the opportunity cost of their time. As a result, in most situations, conducting 30 interviews is easier and less expensive than conducting five focus groups of seven to 10 people.

THE MODIFIED KANO MODEL

One of the difficulties in using interviews or focus groups to obtain customer consequences is getting the customers to tell you all the consequences that are important to them. The problem is that customers do not always think about all the important consequences. Indeed, sometimes they are not even aware of important consequences.

The Kano model helps us understand why consumers do not recognize all the consequences that are important to them. The graphical depiction of the Kano model uses two axes, the degree of providing desired consequences and the level of customer satisfaction, from dissatisfaction to loyalty. Figure 4.1 shows these axes, along with the relationship between these two dimensions for the type of consequences generally known and expressed by customers: performance consequences.

Performance consequences are those consequences that customers currently use to judge service brands. They are the types of consequences on which different brands vary. Often a marketer differentiates a brand based on one or more of these performance consequences and advertises the brand's superiority on them. Thus, these types of consequences are generally the first ones that customers remember and name. Some of these consequences are important to all customers, while others appeal to a specific market segment.

The degree of providing performance consequences is positively and linearly related to the level of customer satisfaction, as depicted by the straight line in Figure 4.1 labeled "Performance consequences." If a brand does not provide these consequences, customers will be very dissatisfied. If

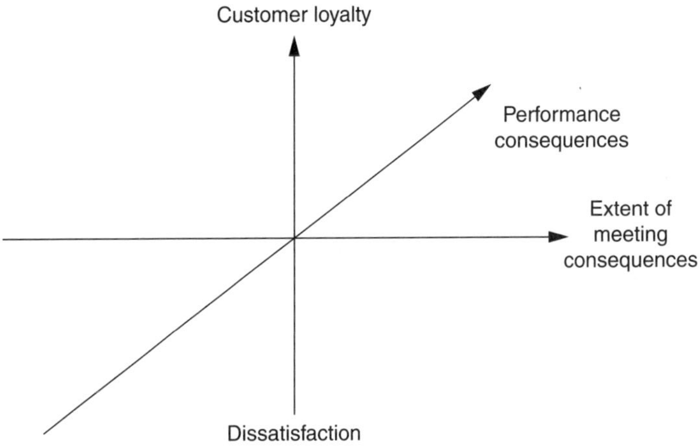

Figure 4.1 Performance consequences.

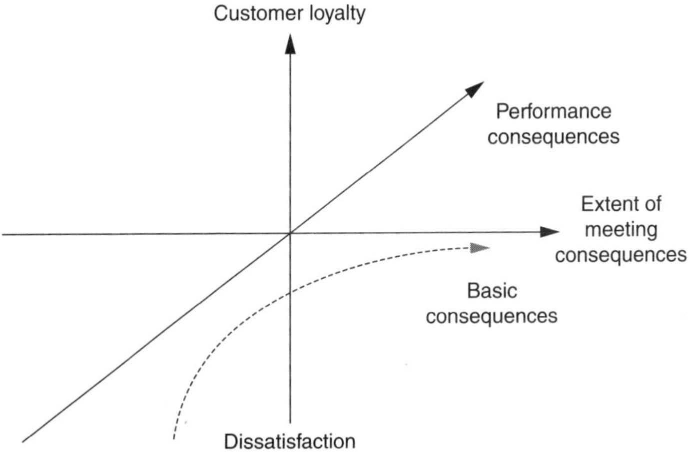

Figure 4.2 Basic consequences.

a brand provides these consequences very well, customers will be very satisfied, perhaps even loyal.

In Figure 4.2, we have added a second line, labeled "Basic consequences." It represents the relationship between degree of providing basic consequences and level of customer satisfaction. Notice that this line is not straight, indicating that this relationship is not linear. When a brand does not provide these basic consequences, customers are very dissatisfied. However, when a brand provides these consequences very well, customers show only moderate levels of satisfaction, being neither dissatisfied nor loyal. Generally, all service providers perform well on these consequences and they provide no competitive advantage.

Basic consequences are those that customers expect of all service brands. These are such things as an airline getting us to our destination or a hotel room having a bed. The reason that customers do not think about these consequences is that they expect them from all service providers. Generally, all brands provide these consequences. Ones that do not provide these consequences go out of business quickly.

Figure 4.3 shows a third line, labeled "Excitement consequences." It represents the relationship between degree of achieving excitement consequences and level of customer satisfaction. Again, this line is not straight and the relationship is not linear. When a brand does not provide these excitement consequences, customers are not dissatisfied. Their level of satisfaction is neutral; they are neither satisfied nor dissatisfied. However, when a brand provides these excitement consequences, customers exhibit very high levels of satisfaction and loyalty.

These excitement consequences are those that no service brand is currently providing, at least as far as the customer is aware. They represent new, cutting-edge consequences that can lead to a tremendous competitive advantage in the marketplace. Examples from the past might be call-forwarding options on a phone or color printers.

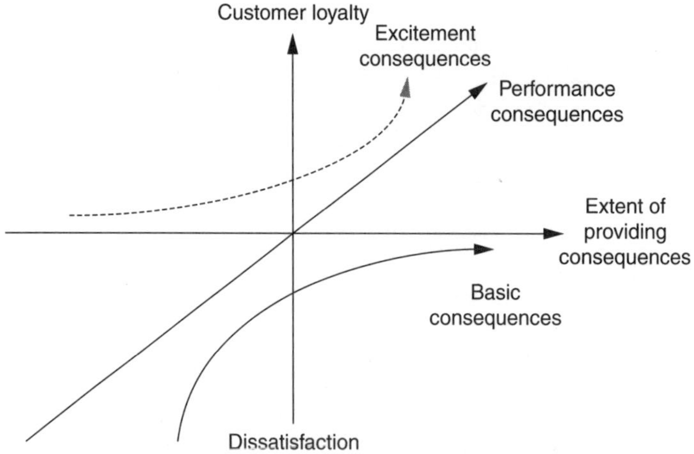

Figure 4.3 Excitement consequences.

We really want to learn about potential excitement consequences, but this is difficult because consumers are not even aware of them themselves. We have to be creative in coming up with these potential competitive advantages based on existing consequences and underlying needs and values of our consumers. One question we use during interviews to try to obtain some of these consequences is, "What would your ideal service be like?" Another is, "What else could this service do for you?" A third is, "Tell me how you use this service." All of these elicit hints of additional consequences. We combine these hints with our knowledge of the services and new technologies to develop new attributes that result in consequences never provided by this type of service in the past.

Identifying the Consequences from the Interview Transcripts

To get all the desired consequences from the tapes or transcripts of the interviews, we have three individuals review them separately and write down every attribute and consequence they detect. Three individuals working independently seem to detect most of the consequences and attributes mentioned, with diminishing returns provided from using a fourth individual.[2] For best results, these individuals need to understand the differences between attributes and consequences, to understand the Kano model, and to understand the importance of obtaining all the consequences.

OTHER SOURCES OF DATA

Using interviews and focus groups to obtain desired consequences is a very important and necessary process. Other sources of consequences are available, however, and we do not ignore them. These sources include industry literature, trade shows, and the knowledge of our own in-house experts. Ask employees who have direct contact with your customers and your operations experts to provide their ideas on consequences desired by your customers. Add these to your list before proceeding to the next step, organizing the customer voice. Other approaches to gathering information on desired consequences are to observe customers using our services or to use mystery shoppers who anonymously use our services and report on their experiences.

ORGANIZING THE CUSTOMER VOICE

We use two different approaches to organize the voice of the customer. In the first, the affinity diagram, the team members sort the consequences desired by the customer. The other approach, the customer sort, has a sample of customers do the sorting. We describe them below.

Affinity Diagram

Before the team gets together to begin the process, write each consequence desired by consumers on a self-adhesive note sheet. Supply a large surface to which the note sheets adhere for use in sorting the consequences.

Next, assemble the team to conduct the process. The team consists of no more than six members from the larger service development team. Explain the affinity diagram process to them. Emphasize that they are to maintain silence throughout the sorting process to encourage creativity. Also, recommend that they move very quickly without thinking too long about any possible pairing or groupings. Just like a brainstorming process, speed avoids censoring ideas and aids creativity.

The team sorts the desired consequences into groupings. Each member looks for consequences that relate to each other in any way and places them near each other on the large surface. Use any pairing that comes to mind. If someone does not like where a consequence is, that person moves it. This process continues until the team has placed all consequences in groupings and team members have stopped moving the consequences around. Depending on the team and the consequences, this process can take considerable time!

Once they have completed the sorting, the team members select a consequence from each group to be the category title, placing it at the top of the group. Try to represent the essence of the category with this title card. This card best represents all cards in the group.

Customer Sort

We give each customer a deck of cards, each bearing one desired consequence. The customer sorts the cards into piles so that each pile represents similar consequences and differs from the other piles in some way. We ask the customer to choose a single consequence from each pile that best represents the desired consequences in the pile. This consequence, called the exemplar, becomes the category title. We keep it in the voice of the customer.

We record the consequences that the customer puts in each pile, along with the exemplar. Calculate the number of times you paired each consequence with every other consequence. You can analyze the data resulting from the customer sorts by hand or use computer software to do a cluster analysis. To do the analysis by hand, create a matrix with the consequences listed both across the columns and down the rows, in the same order. Draw a diagonal line through the cells where a consequence intersects with itself. Now use only the cells above and to the right of the line. Fill in each cell with the number of times you placed the consequence for that row together with the consequence for that column in a pile. The consequences that you paired together most often form the final groupings of consequences.

In general, those who have tried both approaches to grouping consequences say that the customer sort provides a clearer, more believable, easier-to-work-with representation of customer perceptions than the affinity diagram. However, the customer sort approach takes considerably more time to perform.

Once you have completed the groupings, whether through using the affinity diagram or the customer sort, develop a sorted listing of the consequences. Put the first category title flush to the left margin. After it, place every other consequence in the category below it, indented on a separate line. Then go to the next category title and follow the same process. Figure 4.4 shows an example.

Package received when needed.
- Package received the next day.
- Package received in two days.
- Package received before 10 AM.
- Package received on Saturday.
- Package delivered to correct location.
- Package delivered to correct person.
- Package not left outside.
- Package not left with a neighbor.

Package delivered in good condition.
- Package not torn.
- Items sent not damaged.

Pickup service convenient.
- Package picked up at my location.
- Package picked up during my working hours.

Delivery can be tracked.

Figure 4.4 Sorted consequences for delivery services.

FINDING AND ADDING MISSING CONSEQUENCES

Despite all our best efforts at obtaining and sorting the customer voice, we may miss some consequences. We can use a grid to help us find and add missing consequences. The grid starts with the categories of consequences we created above in the first column and then proceeds to the items in the categories. After that, we add columns of more specific consequences and even attributes. Figure 4.5 shows part of a grid for the delivery service example.

Type	General Consequence	Specific Consequence	Feature
Basic	Package received when needed	Package received the next day	Air shipment
		Package received in two days	
		Package received before 10 AM	Early delivery schedule
		Package received on Saturday	Saturday delivery schedule
	Package delivered to correct location	Package delivered to correct person	Driver verifies address and person
		Package not left outside	Driver uses notes requesting delivery information
		Package not left with a neighbor	Driver uses notes requesting delivery information
	Package delivered in good condition	Package not torn	Good equipment
		Items sent not damaged	Careful handling
Performance	Pickup service convenient	Package picked up at my location	Pickup service
		Package picked up during my working hours	
	Delivery can be tracked		Online tracking by number
Excitement			

Figure 4.5 Grid for delivery service.

<table>
<tr><th>Type</th><th>General Consequence</th><th>Specific Consequence</th><th>Feature</th></tr>
<tr><td>Basic</td><td>Phone was answered</td><td></td><td>Automated phone answering system</td></tr>
<tr><td rowspan="7">Performance</td><td rowspan="3">Convenient appointment scheduling</td><td>I was not put on hold</td><td>Number of people answering phone</td></tr>
<tr><td>I was asked few needless questions</td><td>Good training of phone staff</td></tr>
<tr><td>I spent little time on the phone</td><td>Person answering phone handles call</td></tr>
<tr><td rowspan="3">Convenient appointments</td><td>My call was answered quickly</td><td>Automated phone answering system</td></tr>
<tr><td>I had my choice of days and times</td><td>Flexible scheduling</td></tr>
<tr><td>I got an appointment within a week of my call</td><td>Number of appointments</td></tr>
<tr><td>Quick attention when needed</td><td>I was asked if this was an emergency</td><td>Standard question set</td></tr>
<tr><td>Excitement</td><td></td><td></td><td></td></tr>
</table>

Figure 4.6 Grid for doctor's office.

THE DOCTOR'S OFFICE

The staff of the doctor's office created a grid of the consequences they discovered, to look for any missing consequences. They kept the Kano model in mind while completing the grid, shown in Figure 4.6.

EXERCISE

Prepare questions to do in-depth interviews related to pizza delivery.

Interview at least 10 individuals who order pizza delivered; tape your interviews. Use the techniques described in this chapter to uncover their desired consequences. You want to come out of each interview with a list of all the consequences desired by this individual and all the negative consequences that the individual wants to avoid. Be sure to probe for underlying consequences when given an attribute or characteristic of the pizza delivery service, like a 30-minute delivery guarantee. Also, when an individual gives you a consequence without a corresponding attribute, ask about the characteristics that might lead to that consequence.

Listen to your tapes and extract all the attributes or characteristics and all the consequences. Create two lists, one for attributes and another for consequences. Organize the consequences, eliminating duplicates and developing natural groupings of those remaining.

Develop and complete a grid from your interview results and look for any missing consequences.

ENDNOTES

1. Abbie Griffin and John R. Hauser, "The Voice of the Customer," *Marketing Science* 12, no. 1 (1993): 1–26.
2. Ibid.

Chapter 5

The Importance of Importance

CHAPTER TOPICS

- Importance Ratings
- Basics of Measurement
- Alternative Importance Scales

CHAPTER TOOLS

- Rank Order Scale
- Itemized Rating Scale
- Constant Sum Scale
- Anchored Scale

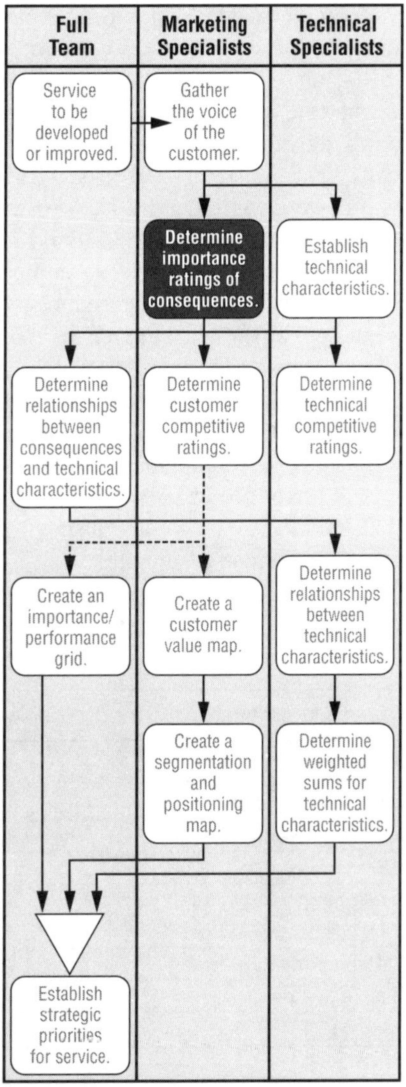

In chapter 3, we introduced the use of customer importance ratings. In this chapter, we show several ways to determine customer importance ratings. First, we need to explain why we want to bother with these ratings. What do they add to the voice of the customer and the customers' ratings of our services?

IMPORTANCE RATINGS

The simple answer is that people place more importance on some consequences than on others. If we weight all consequences equally, we are likely to misinterpret the consumer's overall attitude or satisfaction and poorly predict the consumer's purchase behavior. Let us look at an example for pizza delivery. Table 5.1 shows consumers' ratings of three brands of pizza delivery using six desired consequences.

If we assume that the consumers would choose a pizza based on the most important consequence only, then we'd predict that the consumers would choose brand A. If we assume that all of these consequences are equally important to the consumers, then we would predict that consumers would prefer and would purchase brand B most frequently because the total of its ratings on all consequences is highest. If we include measurement of the relative importance of each of the consequences and use these importance measures to weight the brand ratings, we could get a very different answer, as shown in Table 5.2.

An error people make frequently is to assume that the number of times consumers mention a consequence indicates its importance to them. While this is a common assumption, it is invalid.[1] The Kano model shown in the last chapter illustrates why. Remember that customers usually mention the performance consequences, not the basic or excitement consequences.

Table 5.1 Brand ratings for pizza delivery.

Consequence/Brand	A	B	C
The crust is good	4.1	2.9	3.4
Order is taken quickly	3.6	4.4	4.0
Delivery is quick	2.7	3.5	3.7
I can get my favorite toppings	4.2	3.5	3.5
Pizza is hot when I get it	3.8	4.0	4.1
I can order when I want	3.4	4.5	3.5
I save money	3.0	4.0	4.3
Sum	24.8	26.8	26.5

Table 5.2 Weighted brand ratings for pizza delivery.

Brand:		A		B		C	
Consequence	**Importance Rating**	**Rating**	**Weighted Rating**	**Rating**	**Weighted Rating**	**Rating**	**Weighted Rating**
The crust is good	9.7	4.1	39.77	2.9	28.13	3.4	32.98
Order is taken quickly	6.6	3.6	23.76	4.4	29.04	4.0	26.4
Delivery is quick	8.1	2.7	21.87	3.5	28.35	3.7	29.97
I can get my favorite toppings	7.5	4.2	31.50	3.5	26.25	3.5	26.25
Pizza is hot when I get it	7.8	3.8	29.64	4.0	31.20	4.1	31.98
I can order when I want	6.5	3.4	22.10	4.5	29.25	3.5	22.75
I save money	8.3	3.0	24.90	4.0	33.20	4.3	35.69
Sum	54.5	24.8	193.54	26.8	205.42	26.5	206.02
Average			3.55		3.77		3.78

Because the brands are competing based on the performance consequences, service providers mention these consequences frequently in promotions for the brands. Therefore, they come to the mind of customers most often and consumers mention them most often during interviews or focus groups. On the other hand, consumers may not mention basic consequences very often, even though they are very important—because they are expected. Consumers seldom mention excitement consequences because they are not even aware that they want or could possibly get them.

As a result, we must find a way to measure the importance to consumers of the consequences determined through interviews or focus groups. Before we determine the best measurement method, we need to discuss the basics of measurement scales.

BASICS OF MEASUREMENT

Measurement scales are important because they determine how we can treat our data statistically. Knowing about measurement scales allows us to make intelligent decisions about how to word our questions to get the type of data we need for our analysis.

Measurement scales are of two main types, metric and non-metric. These correspond to two types of statistical tests, metric and non-metric. Metric tests include t-tests, analysis of variance, and linear regression, the tests familiar to most people from college statistics. We would prefer to use metric statistical tests because they are more powerful than non-metric tests; in other words, metric statistical tests detect smaller differences between groups of numbers. We may also use metric measurements for multiplication, something we are going to want to do as we develop new services and select service features.

Both metric and non-metric measurement scales have two subtypes. Metric scales are either interval or ratio scales. Non-metric scales are either nominal or ordinal.

Nominal scales put the items we are measuring into categories or groups. Think of name when you hear nominal—the names of the categories. Common examples of nominal measurement scales used in questionnaires are questions about gender (male or female) or race (Caucasian, African-American, Hispanic, and so on). Both of these question scales place items into categories, but nothing more. The categories have no natural order. The only statistical techniques we can use are frequencies, percentages, and the mode.

Ordinal scales rank order the items we are measuring. Think of order when you hear ordinal. The type of ordinal question most frequently used in questionnaires is one that asks the respondent to indicate agreement with a statement on a scale, such as: strongly disagree, disagree, neutral, agree, strongly agree. Ordinal scales also place the answers into categories, but these categories have order, unlike those in a nominal scale. Statistically, we can use frequencies, percentages, the mode, or the median with ordinal measurement scales.

Interval scales measure items with categories that represent equal-sized intervals. We often measure age and income using interval scales. Each interval must contain the same number of ages or income levels to qualify the scale as interval rather than ordinal. When we have an interval scale, we represent each interval by the middle value in that interval. Then we may multiply the number of cases in the interval by the middle value, and add and subtract values in an interval scale. We may also use the mean when we have interval measurement scales, in addition to frequencies, percentages, modes, and median. Finally, we may use metric statistics like t-tests, analyses of variance, and linear regression with less concern about violating the assumptions of these tests.

Ratio scales have one additional feature that interval scales do not have, an absolute zero value. This feature leads to the ability to say that one value in a ratio scale is a given number of times greater than another value or to multiply and divide the values in a ratio scale. Examples of ratio scales are distance measurements, weight, and sales dollars. We can have zero distance, zero weight, and zero sales dollars. We may say that $10,000 in sales is twice $5000 in sales.

Let us look at an example to demonstrate the differences between these scales more fully. Say we want to create a sheet for an observer to record the length of time taken to answer an incoming phone call. If we want to use a ratio scale, the form would have blank lines for an observer to record the exact length of time taken to answer the call in seconds. A form using an interval scale would have categories for the observer to check for each incoming call. These categories would be equal in size, such as zero to four seconds, five to nine seconds, 10 to 14 seconds, and so on. An ordinal scale would use categories similar to those used in the interval scale, but the categories would not be equal in size. For example, the categories might be zero to nine seconds, 10 to 14 seconds, 15 to 19 seconds, and 20 seconds or more.

A nominal scale to measure the length of time taken to answer a phone call is harder to imagine. Let us say our company wants employees to answer all phone calls in less than 20 seconds. Then our nominal scale might have two categories: "yes," answered within required limits or "no," not answered within required limits. This isn't a perfect example of a nominal scale because we could say that the two categories have order since "yes" is shorter than "no." A better example of a nominal scale, although not really measuring the time to answer a phone call, would be a scale that measured the way each call was answered: by the operator, by voice mail, by the automated service, or not answered.

ALTERNATIVE IMPORTANCE SCALES

Now let's go back to looking at how to measure the importance of a set of consequences desired by consumers. People commonly use four different scales to measure relative importance: rank order, itemized rating, constant sum, and anchored.

The *rank order scale* provides a list of consequences and asks the consumer to rate them in order of importance from one to the number of consequences listed, as shown in Figure 5.1. Consumers have little trouble understanding how to answer rank order questions unless the number of consequences gets large, especially larger than 10. On the other hand, they have no way of ranking two consequences the same if they feel they are equally important. A rank order scale provides an ordinal measurement. The proper measure of the average is the median. We should not use the results to multiply times brand ratings because of the nature of this measurement scale.

Rank the following consequences of pizza delivery from one to seven according to how important they are to you. Give the most important consequence a seven. Then assign numbers to the others to indicate the order of their importance to you.

______ The crust is good
______ My order is taken quickly
______ Delivery is quick
______ I can get my favorite toppings
______ The pizza is hot when I get it
______ I can order when I want
______ I save money

Figure 5.1 Rank order scale.

Rate each of the consequences given below using the scale provided. Circle the number that best represents your feelings about the importance of that consequence.

Consequence	**Not at all important**	**Slightly important**	**Important**	**Very important**	**Extremely important**
The crust is good	1	2	3	4	5
My order is taken quickly	1	2	3	4	5
Delivery is quick	1	2	3	4	5
I can get my favorite toppings	1	2	3	4	5
The pizza is hot when I get it	1	2	3	4	5
I can order when I want	1	2	3	4	5
I save money	1	2	3	4	5

Figure 5.2 Itemized rating scale.

The *itemized rating scale* asks the consumers to rate each consequence on a specified scale of importance, as shown in Figure 5.2. It is easy for the consumer to understand and answer. The consumer may give more than one consequence the same rating. However, the choice of scale item names strongly influences the results. The discrete rating scale provides ordinal measurements. The proper measure of the average is the median. We should not use it in multiplication.

The *constant sum scale* gives the consumer a total number of points that is to be divided among the consequences to indicate their relative importance, as shown in Figure 5.3. Usually, we use 100 points or 100 dollars, making this scale realistic. An advantage over the rank order scale is that the consumer may assign the same number of points to more than one consequence and may assign zero points to one or more consequence. Unfortunately, this scale is more complicated for consumers to use, especially when the number of consequences does not divide evenly into 100. Often they rate each consequence on a scale of 100, making their questionnaire unusable. The constant sum scale provides ratio measurements. We may use the mean as the measure of average, and we may multiply the results times the brand ratings.

The *anchored scale* first asks the consumer to choose the most important consequence from a list and to assign 10 points to that consequence, as shown in Figure 5.4. Then we ask the consumer to rate the importance of all the other consequences in relationship to the most important one on a scale of zero to 10. The consumer may rate more than one consequence the same, allowing equality of importance. Instructions are very important for this type of scale so that every consumer assigns a 10 to at least one consequence—creating the importance anchor. A natural fear when using this scale is that the consumers rate all consequences as high in importance; in the authors' experience, this rarely happens. The anchored scale provides a ratio measurement; we may use the mean as the measure of average, and we may multiply the results times the brand ratings.

Table 5.3 compares these four scales for measuring importance. For our purposes, we want a scale that we may multiply times our brand ratings and

Divide 100 points among the following consequences of pizza delivery to show how important each is to you. You may assign a consequence from 0 to 100 points, just make sure that the total for all consequences equals 100.

_____ The crust is good
_____ My order is taken quickly
_____ Delivery is quick
_____ I can get my favorite toppings
_____ The pizza is hot when I get it
_____ I can order when I want
_____ I save money

Figure 5.3 Constant sum scale.

Find the consequence in the list below that is most important to you. Assign it ten (10) points. Then assign from zero (0) to ten (10) points to the other consequences to indicate how important they are to you in comparison to the one that is most important. You may assign the same number of points to more than one consequence.

______ The crust is good
______ My order is taken quickly
______ Delivery is quick
______ I can get my favorite toppings
______ The pizza is hot when I get it
______ I can order when I want
______ I save money

Figure 5.4 Anchored scale.

Table 5.3 Comparison of scales.

Scale	Measurement Type	Strength	Weakness	Average	Equality	Zero	Multiply
Rank order	Ordinal	Easy to understand	Short lists only	Median	No	No	No
Itemized rating	Ordinal	Easy to answer	Wording critical	Median	Yes	No	No
Constant sum	Ratio	Realistic	Confusing	Mean	Yes	Yes	Yes
Anchored	Ratio	Works with a long list	Anchor critical	Mean	Yes	Yes	Yes

that meets the criteria for metric statistics. Both the constant sum and the anchored scales meet these requirements. The authors prefer the anchored scale because the consumer can apply it easily to long lists of consequences that often occur in service situations, and it is less confusing than the constant sum scale because it does not require the consumer to divide.

THE DOCTOR'S OFFICE

The staff at the doctor's office developed a questionnaire to measure the importance of the consequences their patients wanted, shown in Figure 5.5.

Find the consequence of making an appointment with a doctor in the list below that is most important to you. Assign it ten (10) points. Then assign from zero (0) to ten (10) points to the other consequences to indicate how important they are to you in comparison to the one that is most important. You may assign the same number of points to more than one consequence.

______ I get an appointment within a week of my call
______ I am not put on hold
______ I am asked few needless questions
______ I have my choice of days and times
______ I spend little time on the phone

Figure 5.5 Questionnaire for doctor's office.

Table 5.4 Mean rating for each consequence.

Consequence	Mean Rating
I get an appointment within a week of my call	7.9
I am not put on hold	7.3
I am asked few needless questions	6.8
I have my choice of days and times	9.6
I spend little time on the phone	8.2

For a week, they asked every patient who visited the office to complete the survey. Table 5.4 shows the average rating for each consequence.

EXERCISE

Create a questionnaire using an anchored scale to measure the importance of the consequences of pizza delivery you determined in chapter 4. Administer the questionnaire to as many consumers as possible; you would like to get at least 40 responses.

Enter the responses into Microsoft Excel or a statistical software package. Calculate the average (mean) importance rating for each consequence.

ENDNOTE

1. Robert B. Woodruff and Sarah F. Gardial, *Know Your Customer: New Approaches to Understanding Customer Value and Satisfaction* (Cambridge, MA: Blackwell Publishers, 1996).

Chapter 6

Customer Competitive Analysis

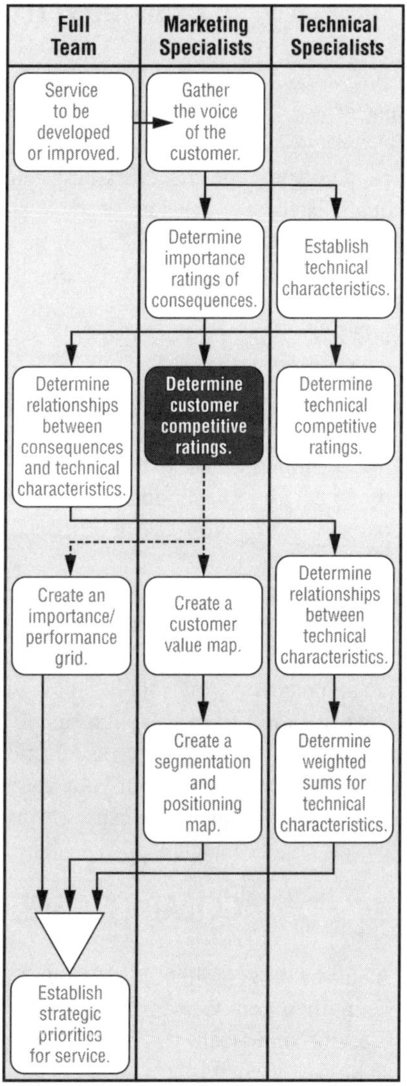

CHAPTER TOPICS

- Competitive Ratings
- Competitive Comparison
- Verifying Your Data
- Placement in the Quality House

CHAPTER TOOLS

- Likert Scales
- Brand Ratings
- Competitive Profile
- Verification by Weighting

Now we know what consequences consumers are looking for (chapter 4) and how important each of these consequences is to them (chapter 5). In this chapter, we learn how to do a competitive evaluation. The competitive evaluation has customers rate our service and the services of our key competitors on the delivery of the consequences that they desire. This competitive evaluation helps us turn our data into information that is useful for strategic decision making.

COMPETITIVE RATINGS

The *competitive analysis* compares our delivery of desired consequences to that of our key competitors. Typically, we use a Likert-type scale of five points to measure customer beliefs for each organization. Likert scales are ordinal scales; the distances between the points on the scale may not be equal. The proper measure of the average is the median. The Likert scale is not metric, so we are breaking basic assumptions when we use metric statistics. Luckily, these statistics are not that sensitive to this type of failure; researchers have found the use of metric statistics with Likert scales to be valid over many years of use.

Figure 6.1 shows how the Likert-type scale would be set up for the competitive analysis using the pizza delivery service from chapter 5.

Administer this questionnaire to as many customers as possible. If you have a limited number of businesses as customers, then you may want to administer the questionnaire to a number of different employees at each business who your service impacts, including purchasing, the decision maker, and the users.

Calculate the average for each brand on each consequence for comparison purposes. The technically correct measure of the average for Likert-type scales is the median. You may, and many people do, calculate the mean; however, you should not consider small differences often found between brand means as significant. In other words, if your brand has a mean on one consequence of 4.2 and your competitor has a mean of 4.4, you should not assume that your competitor is significantly better at delivering that consequence because of the ordinal nature of the scale.

COMPETITIVE COMPARISON

Once you have collected the data and calculated the averages for each brand, then you want to compare the brands. We are not interested in statistically significant differences at this point, so we do not conduct any

For each brand below, circle the number that best indicates how well you feel it satisfies each of the items listed. Use a scale of:

1 = Strongly disagree
2 = Disagree
3 = Neutral
4 = Agree
5 = Strongly agree

	Brand A	Brand B	Brand C
The crust is good	1 2 3 4 5	1 2 3 4 5	1 2 3 4 5
My order is taken quickly	1 2 3 4 5	1 2 3 4 5	1 2 3 4 5
Delivery is quick	1 2 3 4 5	1 2 3 4 5	1 2 3 4 5
I can get my favorite toppings	1 2 3 4 5	1 2 3 4 5	1 2 3 4 5
The pizza is hot when I get it	1 2 3 4 5	1 2 3 4 5	1 2 3 4 5
I can order when I want	1 2 3 4 5	1 2 3 4 5	1 2 3 4 5
I save money	1 2 3 4 5	1 2 3 4 5	1 2 3 4 5

Figure 6.1 Competitive rating questionnaire for pizza delivery.

statistical tests, although we could do so. Instead, we want to be able to compare the brands easily to aid our decisions. A visual depiction is easier to understand quickly, so we convert the averages into a visual representation called the competitive profile.[1]

The *competitive profile* uses a letter or symbol for each brand and places the symbol underneath the median score obtained by that brand on each consequence. We place the consequences in separate rows. We often put the mean importance ratings right in the competitive profile for easy access. Let us look at an example for pizza delivery using the data from Table 5.1, repeated below in Table 6.1.

Next, we convert this data into the visual competitive profile, as shown in Table 6.2. We plot each brand's rating on a consequence below the numbers to approximate its position. We put a rating of 2.0 directly under the two. We put a rating of 2.9 next to the line dividing two from three. In this case, we used A, B, and C to represent the brands.

Once we have completed plotting the ratings for each brand on every consequence, we can interpret the results. We look for gaps: gaps between our brand and the competition and gaps between our brand and the highest

Table 6.1 Brand ratings for pizza delivery.

Consequences	Mean Importance	Brand		
		A	B	C
The crust is good	9.7	4.1	2.9	3.4
Order is taken quickly	6.6	3.6	4.4	4.0
Delivery is quick	8.1	2.7	3.5	3.7
I can get my favorite toppings	7.5	4.2	3.5	3.5
Pizza is hot when I get it	7.8	3.8	4.0	4.1
I can order when I want	6.5	3.4	4.5	3.5
I save money	8.3	3.0	4.0	4.3

Table 6.2 Competitive profile for pizza delivery.

Consequences	Mean Importance	Average Rating				
		1	2	3	4	5
The crust is good	9.7		B	C	A	
Order is taken quickly	6.6			A	C B	
Delivery is quick	8.1		A	BC		
I can get my favorite toppings	7.5			BC	A	
Pizza is hot when I get it	7.8			A	BC	
I can order when I want	6.5			AC	B	
I save money	8.3			A	B C	

possible score, 5.0. If our brand is A, then we are behind the competition overall and have a higher price. This combination does not bode well for our future survival!

We can see that we are ahead of the competition on "The crust is good" and on "I can get my favorite toppings." On "The crust is good," we still have a considerable gap between our rating and the highest possible. Since this consequence is most important to consumers, we would want to improve our crust. This is a priority item for us. Our crust may be keeping us in business, but we do not want to depend on meeting this consequence alone.

Brand A is behind the competition on "Order is taken quickly," "Delivery is quick," "I can order when I want," and "I save money." "Delivery is quick" and "I save money" are more important to customers than the other two, although not as important as "The crust is good." These would both be high priority items to work on providing. We should look at our delivery speed and at our pricing.

VERIFYING YOUR DATA

At this point, you have gathered the voice of the customer, turned it into consequences, had customers rate the importance of these consequences, and had customers rate three brands on their delivery of these consequences. This data can be very useful, but only if it is validly measuring what you wanted to measure. Before you use this data to make strategic decisions, you would probably like to verify its validity. Happily, an easy method exists for doing so.

The key to verifying the data is to have something against which to verify it. One approach is to add an overall satisfaction question ("Overall, I am satisfied with this brand") at the end of your Likert-type scales for measuring brand ratings. If your importance weightings and brand ratings are good measures, they should correlate with overall satisfaction for each brand. To test this, we create an average weighted rating for each brand.

For the first brand, multiply the brand rating on a consequence by the appropriate importance rating for that consequence. Do the same for each consequence, then sum these weighted ratings together to get the sum of weighted ratings for that brand. Repeat for each brand. Note that this sum is the same as the sum of weighted ratings in Table 5.2, reproduced as Table 6.3. Then we divide these sums of weighted ratings by the sum of the importance ratings to get the average weighted ratings.

Table 6.3 Weighted brand ratings for pizza delivery.

	Brand:	A		B		C	
Consequence	**Importance Rating**	**Rating**	**Weighted Rating**	**Rating**	**Weighted Rating**	**Rating**	**Weighted Rating**
The crust is good	9.7	4.1	39.77	2.9	28.13	3.4	32.98
Order is taken quickly	6.6	3.6	23.76	4.4	29.04	4.0	26.4
Delivery is quick	8.1	2.7	21.87	3.5	28.35	3.7	29.97
I can get my favorite toppings	7.5	4.2	31.50	3.5	26.25	3.5	26.25
Pizza is hot when I get it	7.8	3.8	29.64	4.0	31.20	4.1	31.98
I can order when I want	6.5	3.4	22.10	4.5	29.25	3.5	22.75
I save money	8.3	3.0	24.90	4.0	33.20	4.3	35.69
Sum	54.5	24.8	193.54	26.8	205.42	26.5	206.02
Average			3.55		3.77		3.78

Verify your data by calculating the correlation between the average weighted rating and the overall satisfaction for each brand. A quicker way of checking the validity of your data is to compare the order of the brands on average overall satisfaction (all consumers) with their order on the average weighted ratings (all consumers). If brand A is highest on overall satisfaction, then it should have the highest average weighted rating. One brand should also be lowest on both. Looking again at Table 5.2, brand C had the highest average weighted rating, and brand A had the lowest. We would expect brand C to have the highest overall satisfaction rating, and brand A to have the lowest. While not a very sophisticated measure of validity, this technique offers a simplicity that makes it easy to communicate to others.

PLACEMENT IN THE QUALITY HOUSE

The information in Table 6.2 comprises the customer section of the quality house in quality function deployment. It represents the horizontal portion of the house, except for the matrix that shows the relationships between the customer consequences and the technical requirements. Table 6.4 shows this portion of the house with space left in the middle for the relationship matrix. Of course, the actual relationship matrix would be much larger since we would have far more than seven consequences and four technical requirements in reality.

Table 6.4 Customer section of the quality house.

Customer Consequence	**Importance Weight**	**Requirements**				**Customer Competitive Profile**				
						1	**2**	**3**	**4**	**5**
The crust is good	9.7						B	C	A	
Order is taken quickly	6.6							A	C B	
Delivery is quick	8.1						A	BC		
I can get my favorite toppings	7.5							BC	A	
Pizza is hot when I get it	7.8							A	BC	
I can order when I want	6.5							AC	B	
I save money	8.3							A	B C	

THE DOCTOR'S OFFICE

The staff at the doctor's office developed a questionnaire to measure the importance of the consequences their patients wanted and to measure patients' perceptions of how the office delivered those consequences. For comparison purposes, the questionnaire asked the patients to rate another office, either another doctor or a dentist, on its delivery performance as well. Figure 6.2 shows their questionnaire.

Find the consequence of making an appointment with a doctor in the list below that is most important to you. Assign it ten (10) points. Then assign from zero (0) to ten (10) points to the other consequences to indicate how important they are to you in comparison to the most important one. You may assign the same number of points to more than one consequence.

______ I get an appointment within a week of my call
______ I am not put on hold
______ I am asked few needless questions
______ I have my choice of days and times
______ I spend little time on the phone

Please rate how well we deliver each of these consequences when you call to set up an appointment. Circle the number below that best indicates how well you feel we satisfy each of the consequences. For comparison purposes, please rate another office on the same consequences; rate either another doctor's office or a dentist's office that you have visited in the past year. Use a scale of:

1 = Strongly disagree
2 = Disagree
3 = Neutral
4 = Agree
5 = Strongly agree

	Our Office	Another Office
I get an appointment within a week of my call	1 2 3 4 5	1 2 3 4 5
I am not put on hold	1 2 3 4 5	1 2 3 4 5
I am asked few needless questions	1 2 3 4 5	1 2 3 4 5
I have my choice of days and times	1 2 3 4 5	1 2 3 4 5
I spend little time on the phone	1 2 3 4 5	1 2 3 4 5
Overall, I am satisfied with the appointment process	1 2 3 4 5	1 2 3 4 5

Figure 6.2 Questionnaire for doctor's office.

They asked every patient who came into the office during the next week to complete the questionnaire while waiting to see the doctor. A staff member entered the data into Microsoft Excel and calculated weighted ratings and averages. Table 6.5 shows the results. The average weighted ratings are virtually equal, not in agreement with the overall satisfaction ratings, where the doctor's office scored higher than the competitors' offices. Two reasons for this disagreement are possible. First, some important consequence could be missing or some other wording problem could exist. Perhaps someone reworded the consequences incorrectly. Second, the use of a variety of offices for the comparison measure could account for the disagreement. Using a variable comparison office would lead to greater variability in the data and could well account for the disagreement in this situation.

The staff created the competitive profile shown in Table 6.6 using A for their office and B for the combination of other offices rated. They were very pleased with their performance on offering a variety of days and times, which was most important to their patients. They were also pleased with their performance on providing an appointment within a week of the call, although they thought they could improve a little in this area. A major area for work was the amount of time the patient had to spend on the phone to get an appointment. It was the second most important consequence, and the office did not rate well on it in an absolute sense or in comparison to the other offices rated. This rating may relate to the rating on asking needless

Table 6.5 Weighted brand ratings for doctor's office.

Brand:		Our Office		Other Offices	
Consequence	**Importance**	**Rating**	**Weighted Rating**	**Rating**	**Weighted Rating**
I get an appointment within a week of my call	7.9	4.2	33.18	2.9	22.91
I am not put on hold	7.3	3.5	25.55	4.4	32.12
I am asked few needless questions	6.8	2.6	17.68	3.4	23.12
I have my choice of days and times	9.6	4.5	43.20	3.5	33.60
I spend little time on the phone	8.2	3.2	26.24	4.2	34.44
Overall, I am satisfied with the appointment process		3.8		3.4	
Sum	39.8	21.8	145.85	21.8	146.19
Average			3.7		3.7

Table 6.6 Competitive profile for the doctor's office.

Consequence	Mean Importance	Average Rating				
		1	2	3	4	5
I get an appointment within a week of my call	7.9		B		A	
I am not put on hold	7.3			A	B	
I am asked few needless questions	6.8		A	B		
I have my choice of days and times	9.6			B	A	
I spend little time on the phone	8.2			A	B	
Overall I am satisfied with the appointment process				B A		

questions during the appointment call. Although it was the least important to their patients, the office rated low in this area. This could be a source of irritation to patients calling in for an appointment in addition to extending the call length.

EXERCISE

Develop a questionnaire repeating the anchored scale you developed in chapter 5 and writing Likert-type scales to measure consumers' perceptions of how brands deliver the consequences you determined in chapter 4. Add a question at the end to measure overall satisfaction. Administer the questionnaire to as many customers as possible. Again, you would like to get at least 40 responses; 100 would be better if you are going to actually use the data to make strategic decisions.

Enter the responses into Microsoft Excel or a statistical software package. Determine the average (mean) rating of each brand on each consequence and on overall satisfaction. Create a competitive profile. Run a Pearson product-moment correlation between the sum of weighted ratings and the overall satisfaction for each brand. Calculate a sum of weighted ratings for each customer for each brand. Make a table comparing each brand's score on the sum of weighted ratings with its score on overall satisfaction. Is your data valid?

ENDNOTE

1. Robert B. Woodruff and Sarah F. Gardial, *Know Your Customer: New Approaches to Understanding Customer Value and Satisfaction* (Cambridge, MA: Blackwell Publishers, 1996).

Part II

Technical Requirements (QFD)

Chapter 7

Technical Characteristics

CHAPTER TOPICS

- Generating the Technical Requirements
- Organizing the Technical Information
- Customer Design Matrix Log
- Developing the Quality House

CHAPTER TOOLS

- Brainstorming
- Tree Diagram
- Customer Design Matrix Log
- Cause-and-Effect Analysis
- Quality House

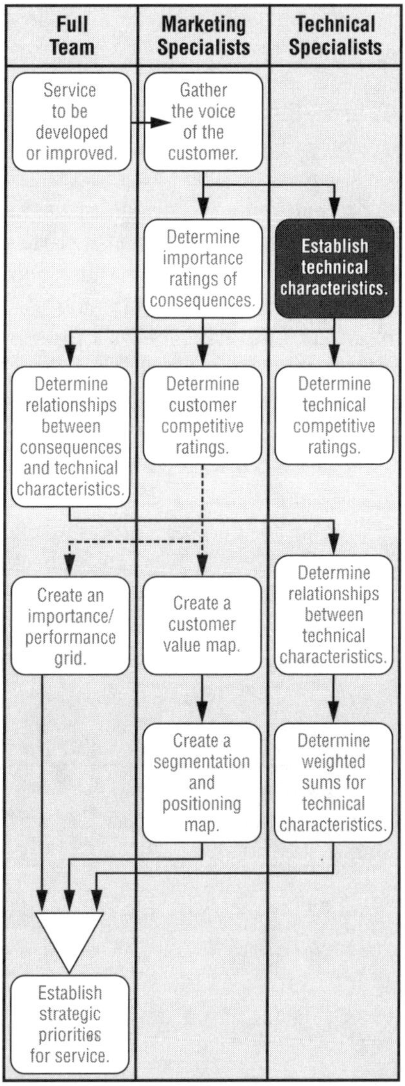

This chapter covers the process used to develop the technical requirements that will satisfy the customer needs for the service or product. A cross-functional design team determines the technology available, the materials requirements, the capability of processes, and the feasibility of concepts; and it evaluates the technical trade-offs. The design team consists of some combination of design engineers, industrial engineers, materials engineers, chemical engineers, process engineers, quality engineers, safety engineers, manufacturing engineers, stylists, suppliers, customers, and purchasing agents. In the service setting, the design team usually consists of employees who are familiar with process design, if not participating in the specific service process that they are studying, along with suppliers, customers, and purchasing agents. The design team determines the feasibility of achieving the process, technical features, and functions. This may require use of brainstorming or feasibility block diagrams.

Customer input is required to select the technical characteristics and properly develop the design of the service, process, or product. The left-hand side of the quality house starts with the weighted or prioritized customer needs (the *whats*). These needs are the consequences defined in chapters 3 and 4. The weighting of the customers' needs helps us in the selection of the critical issues for the technical requirements that we must meet in order to satisfy the customers' needs.[1] These weightings, in turn, determine the weightings for the technical requirements. At this point, we have established the customer section of the house, as shown in Figure 7.1.

Chapter 5 discussed the establishment of the customer rankings or ratings of their needs. An error frequently made at this point is to assume that the number of times consumers mention a consequence indicates its importance to consumers. If you refer back to Table 5.1, you will note that two different evaluations of the consumer's choice for a brand of pizza result in two different scenarios. This is why the initiation of the voice of the customer process is important. The customers' input to the process greatly affects the outcome.

Voice of the customer	Importance ranking	Matrix	Customer complaints or warranty info	Customer competitive info

Figure 7.1 Example of the process to this point.

GENERATING THE TECHNICAL REQUIREMENTS

The team may use a brainstorming methodology for the development of ideas for the technical requirements. This produces many different and varied ideas. For the brainstorming process to work, we state the customers' desired consequences as clearly as possible and develop the alternatives based on those statements of the consequences. This requires close attention to the brainstorming rules and facilitation by someone who has experience with the process. If you have not used brainstorming before, consult an expert. We list the basic phases and rules here for reference for those with experience.

The three phases of brainstorming are:

- The generation phase is where the team generates ideas to achieve a new service or process or enhancement of an existing process.
- The clarification phase is where the team reviews the generated list to group similar ideas and clarify the combined list.
- The third phase is where the team eliminates duplicates, removes irrelevant ideas, and puts aside issues or ideas that are off-limits.

The rules of the brainstorming process for the initial list generation are:

1. State the purpose or problem clearly and briefly before you hold the meeting, preferably 24 hours ahead of time.
2. Call on the individuals to generate and express ideas in sequence and list all ideas without critiquing them. (Select appropriate individuals.)
3. Allow each person to offer only one thought at a time.
4. Do not criticize ideas.
5. Do not discuss ideas at this time.
6. Build on the ideas of others.
7. Record all ideas where they are visible to the team.
8. Once the list is complete, have the team group like ideas and eliminate those that do not support the problem definition.

The team must formulate the technical characteristics required for meeting each customer consequence. We list the technical requirements that we need to accomplish for the customer (often called *hows*) across the top

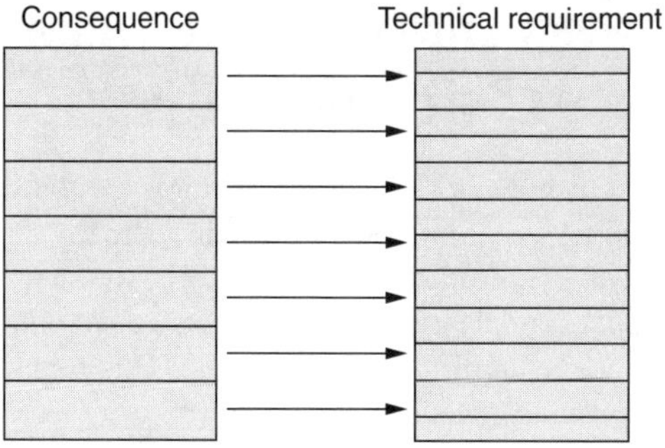

Figure 7.2 Provide one or more hows for each what.

of the house similar to how we listed the customers' needs on the left side. We must match each customer need by specific capabilities to meet those needs, as Figure 7.2 illustrates. If more than one technical requirement can help fulfill the need, we consider each for the analysis. We set a goal of creating one to three technical requirements for each consequence. More gives us too many technical requirements to handle; less will not adequately provide for satisfying customers.[2]

Each technical requirement is a way to meet the corresponding consequence desired by our customers. Each needs to be within our control, an attribute we can vary within our service or process. Each also needs to be measurable so we can set objectives and determine if we are meeting them.

ORGANIZING THE TECHNICAL INFORMATION

We use a creative process to organize the technical information that helps assure that we properly develop and define the technical requirements. The *tree diagram*[3] is a good tool for the development of the specific technical features that help meet the requirements of the customers for the service. We cover the tree diagram process for generating the technical requirements next.

We use the tree diagram to create requirements similar to how we use the cause-and-effect diagram to generate root causes. Figure 7.3 shows a template for a three-layer tree diagram. The tree diagram is useful to link the want or consequence to the technical requirements while performing the analysis. We list the rules to build a tree diagram on the next page.

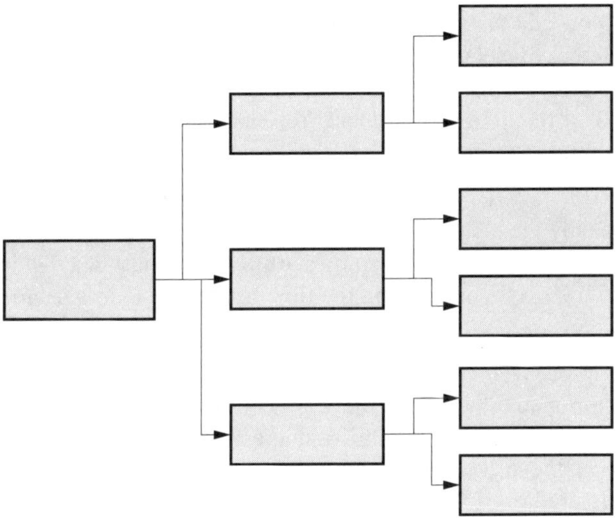

Figure 7.3 Three-layer tree diagram.

Rules for a Successful Tree Diagram

1. Choose one grouping from the completed affinity diagram of customer wants to expand into a tree diagram. (Each group can become the basis for a separate tree diagram.)
2. Agree upon one statement that clearly expresses the core issue, problem, or goal for the group selected. We can use the header card directly from the affinity diagram if it meets the team's approval.
3. Once we identify this primary goal or issue card, we place it on the left side of a flipchart or table.
4. Identify all the elements or components related to this primary statement. Then brainstorm additional elements or components, using the existing card as a starting point. Record each new idea on an index card.
5. Identify the ideas most closely related to the central statement. Arrange them in a column to the right of the central statement, similar to a family tree or organization chart. These ideas represent the secondary level of detail on the diagram.

6. Now add the elements related to this secondary level, to create a tertiary level of detail. Continue until you have added all of the cards or recorded ideas to the diagram in a sequence that shows their relative level of detail. You may find a card does not belong on this tree diagram or that you need a new card to meet the specific goal or purpose.
7. Study the diagram for any holes in the sequence or the logic. You may review each branch by starting at the most detailed item on the far right and tracing the flow from more to less detail.

Reference appendix C for more details on the tree diagram.

The process to develop customer requirements for the technical information matrix is to take the wants or consequences and align them with technical concepts.[4] We illustrate the results of this process for pizza delivery in the following example. Customers want hot, good tasting pizza delivered on-time to their houses. The specific customer needs and expectations are:

- The pizza is cut all the way through the dough.
- The pizza is hot.
- The pizza tastes good.
- The pizza is done all the way.
- There are distinct sauce flavors and spices used.
- The pizza is good every time.
- The pizza does not droop when picked up to eat.
- There is a variety of types available.
- The sauce covers all of the dough.
- The pieces are cut uniformly.
- There are many choices for toppings.
- The sauce is not watery.
- The pizza is not stuck to the box bottom or the paper.
- The pizza is not doughy.
- The pizza is not greasy.
- Generous toppings are supplied.
- Generous cheese is provided.

- Fast delivery.
- Large topping pieces are provided.

The hot pizza delivery needs in Figure 7.4 can be shown using the tree diagram in Figure 7.5.

Quick response	_____ Time to respond (cycle time)
	_____ Time to complete transaction
	_____ Time to deliver
Clean facility	_____ Cleanliness standards
Hot pizza	_____ Hot core bags
	_____ Speedy delivery
	_____ Cook at location
	_____ Cook on way
Fast delivery	_____ Air express
	_____ Automatic sorting
	_____ Hand delivery

Figure 7.4 The pizza house delivery service needs example.

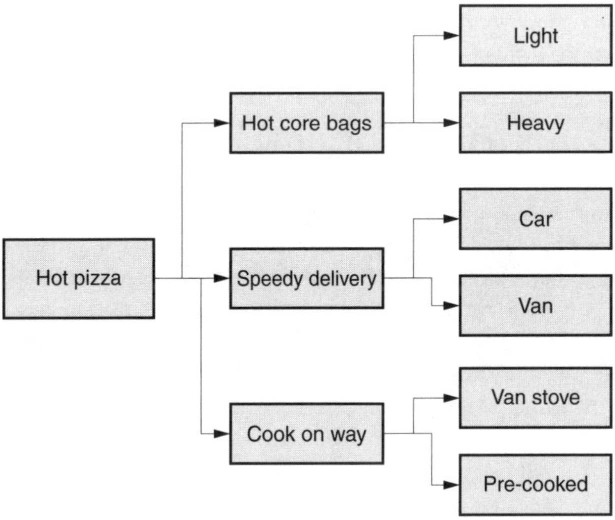

Figure 7.5 The tree diagram for developing technical ideas for a hot pizza.

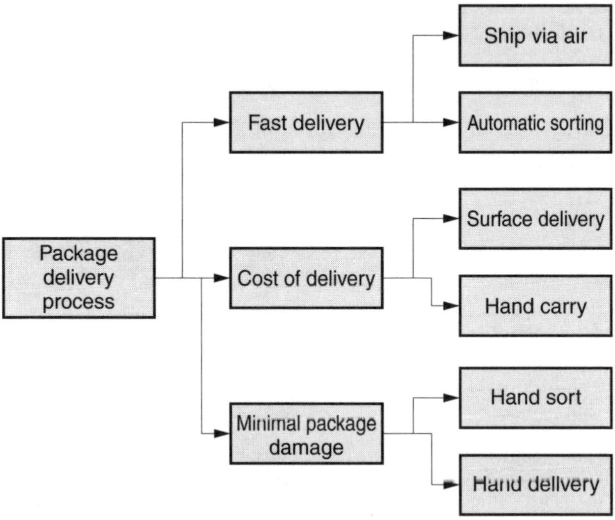

Figure 7.6 An example of a tree diagram for delivery of a package.

Another example of the tree diagram is shown in Figure 7.6. For service processes, such as delivering a package, we need to offer alternatives that provide speedy and safe delivery, based on a given price. The alternatives can be air, surface truck, small service car, bicycle, or a variety of hand deliveries. We must follow up on each of these ideas for feasibility before we consider them for inclusion in the technical requirements of the quality house.

CUSTOMER DESIGN MATRIX LOG

The customer design matrix log[5] creates a product development log and provides a history of the design process. It lists the design concepts that came from the customer's voice and provides detailed design considerations (see Figure 7.7). We fill out the log starting with the concept ideas for the service process or product we are developing. We generate the ideas and list the methods of fulfilling the needs of the customer. The log provides a base for reference as we progress through the conceptual design phases.

A tool that we can use here to help fill in the log is the cause-and-effect diagram. It is useful to generate the technical requirements and can stimulate new ideas.

The cause-and-effect diagram shows the effect desired or the problem to solve. As shown in Figure 7.8, we use six major categories as areas of

No.	Customers' Voice	Technical Requirements	Measuring Units	Value
1	Quick delivery	Drop-off points	Location	Direct
		Air	Planes	Direct
		Ground	Trucks	Direct
2	Low cost	Shipping alternatives	Dollars	Direct

Figure 7.7 Customer design matrix with measuring units and value of the measure for fulfilling customer needs.

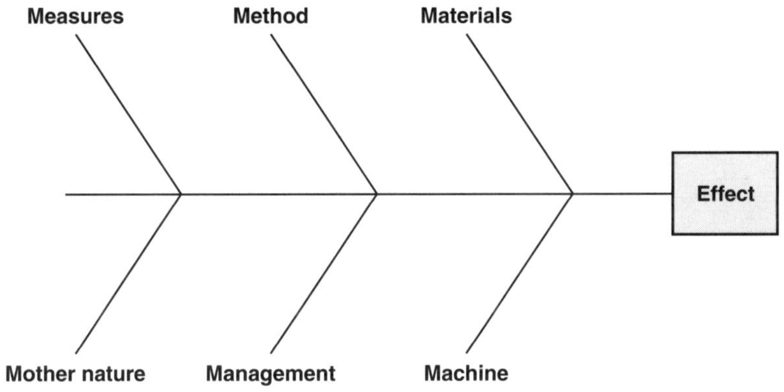

Figure 7.8 Cause-and-effect diagram—the six Ms.

concern or potential factors related to a process to help us generate the causes, associated actions, or areas to consider. (See appendix A for methods on how to build and use a cause-and-effect analysis process.) Figure 7.9 illustrates the cause-and-effect diagram for the the weather effects on a product.

We follow the concepts and steps described above to develop the technical hows for every customer need and expectation that we obtained from the voice-of-the-customer process. The cause-and-effect and brainstorming processes allow for creation of alternative approaches to solving customer needs developed from the voice process. Figures 7.10 and 7.11 show tree diagrams for the pizza delivery example.

The technical staff verifies the company's capability to deliver the technical requirements. This can only be accomplished when the team has the skills that can represent materials sciences, process flow, manufacturing

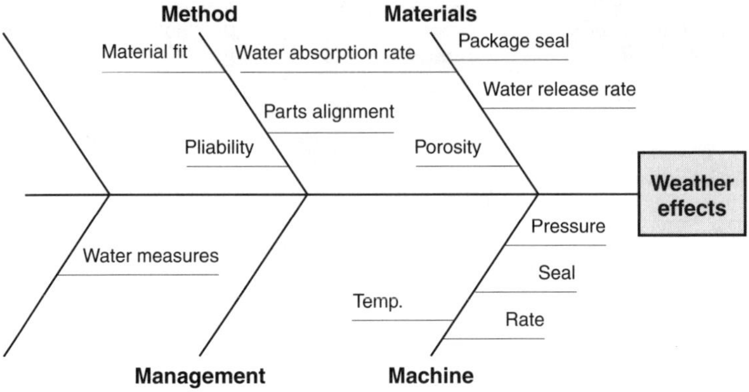

Figure 7.9 Cause-and-effect diagram for weather effects.

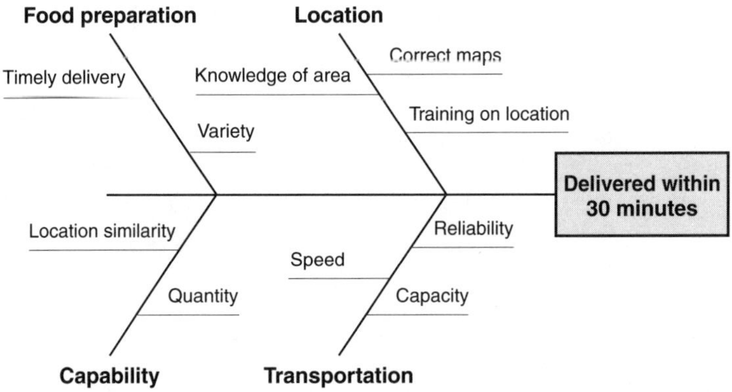

Figure 7.10 Cause-and-effect diagram for the fast delivery of pizza.

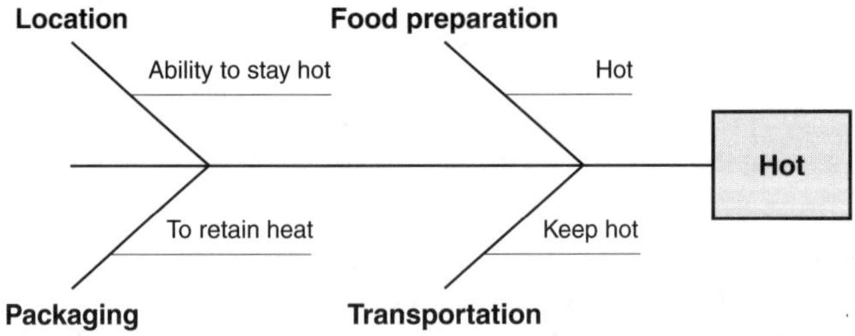

Figure 7.11 Cause-and-effect diagram for the delivery of hot pizza.

capability, process capability, new technologies, supplier capabilities, and mechanical/electronic design capability. In determining the relationships between customer needs and technical requirements, sometimes we need to test features, build prototypes, and/or provide for a validation process. When establishing a "how" in the technical section, always ask how you can measure it before settling on the technical requirement.

DEVELOPING THE QUALITY HOUSE

Once we have completed the technical hows, we work on the relationships for the technical portion of the quality house. We go further in understanding the alternatives if we create a matrix of customer needs to possible technical requirements. This matrix process leads to alternatives that you can discuss with the design team before moving on with the selection of the key design concepts that have the ability to meet the needs of the customer. In the next chapter, we develop the strengths of the relationships between the technical requirements and the customer consequences. The symbols used to indicate the strength of the relationship are:

None	= No relationship	Weight = 0
△	= Small relationship	Weight = 1
○	= Medium relationship	Weight = 3
⊙	= Strong relationship	Weight = 9

We compare all relationships between the voices of the customer (needs) to the technical requirements (hows). Once we have completed this relationship matrix, we evaluate it for technical hows with no relationship to any of the wants (needs) of the customer. We need to question and eliminate these, if possible. This matrix will also point out if we created too many requirements, or hows, during brainstorming. We should have filled in no more than 50 percent of the blocks and should have created a random pattern of filled-in blocks.[6] If this occurs, we will have to select the best choice of requirements to meet the customer needs.

THE DOCTOR'S OFFICE

From the consequences developed in chapter three and the importance ratings developed in chapter 4, the technical staff develops the requirements to meet the needs of the patients. They and the doctors consider the processes that support the customer needs and develop the requirements for the process and the key measures for the process to be successful.

The list of needs obtained from chapter 3 are:

- Length of time until appointment.
- Number of rings until the call is answered.
- Time on hold.
- I was not passed from person to person.
- I was asked few needless questions.
- Use of automated phone system.
- Short waiting time in office.
- Fast response.
- Insurance coverage processing properly.
- Insurance company recognized by office.

From this list of attributes, the following consequences were developed:

- I got an appointment within a week of my call.
- I had my choice of days.
- I had my choice of times.
- I spent little time on the phone.
- I was asked if this was an emergency.
- I was not put on hold.
- I was in the doctor's office on schedule.
- My questions were answered accurately and timely.
- My insurance claim was processed properly.
- My insurance carrier provides coverage for the doctor.

Once you have developed the customer consequences from the voice of the customer and weighted them, you can fill in the left side of the house.

A receptionist handles the customer's need for an appointment with a doctor for a routine check-up or for a diagnosis of a health problem. Since the receptionist has a variety of options, she/he must determine which one or combination of doctors to assign to perform the routine exam or diagnose the patient's problem. The development team must work to identify all the alternatives that exist for questioning the patient, and it must select the method that the receptionist will use to address the customer's needs. Team consensus helps in this process. For the appointment, they offer alternative dates and times. Figure 7.12 shows the quality house with the customers' desired consequences and the weightings the customers assigned to them.

The office personnel develop the processes to handle the consequences desired by the customer. First, they translate the customers' needs (consequences and attributes) into technical requirements using the brainstorming process. Figure 7.13 shows the results of their brainstorming process.

Their next step is to organize the technical requirements using a tree diagram. Figure 7.14 shows part of the tree diagram they developed. The tree diagram is also useful to describe which methods or techniques are

Technical requirements / Customer consequences	Weighting														
Time to appointment	8														
Number of rings	8														
Choice of days	9														
Choice of times	5														
Short time to schedule	9														
Criticalness of visit determined	10														
Appointment made without interruption	5														
Appointment time kept	8														
All questions answered	9														
Insurance claims processed	8														
Insurance coverage recognized	10														

Figure 7.12 Quality house matrix with customer input and importance weightings.

Time to appointment	Availability of doctor
	Type of care required
	Time required during visit
Number of rings	Responsiveness
	Phone locations
	Answering system
Choice of days	Doctors' flexibility
	Number of open slots
	Scheduler flexibility
Choice of times	Doctors' flexibility
	Number of open slots
	Scheduler flexibility
Short time to schedule	Scheduler availability
	Systems capability
Criticalness of visit	Asking the right questions
	Determining the patient needs
No interruptions	Scheduler has the time
	System speed
	Scheduler capability
Appointment time kept	Doctors' availability
	Scheduler system capability
	Doctors' performance
Questions answered	Doctors' performance
	System scheduler capability
	Doctors' accuracy
Insurance claims processed	Systems scheduler capacity
	Scheduler capability
Insurance coverage	Scheduler capability

Figure 7.13 Results of brainstorming technical concepts.

required to satisfy the specific technical requirement chosen to fill the need. The same type of technical information can be obtained using the cause-and-effect diagram. Refer to Figure 7.15 for the appointment process.

Now the team must evaluate the process that meets the selected requirements and determine if a measurement can be developed for each process. The methods used for this are to brainstorm the requirements of the process and choose the process that will meet the needs of the customer. The team

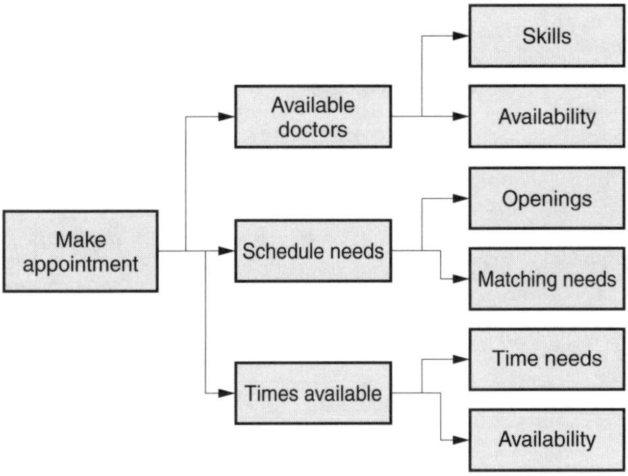

Figure 7.14 The tree diagram example for the doctor's office.

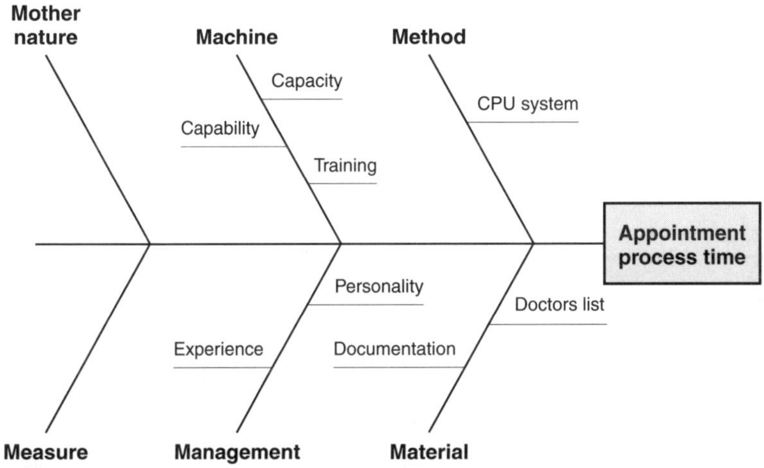

Figure 7.15 The cause-and-effect diagram for doctors' appointments.

then fills in the top of the house. Figure 7.16 is an example of some of the technical requirements, measurements, and values.

The technically key characteristics or considerations are: friendliness, time to obtain appointment, able to help, knowledge about the problem, and courteous. Using this material and information helps us build the quality

No.	Customers' Voice	Technical Requirements	Measuring Units	Value
1	No waiting in office	Scheduler	Time	Seconds
		Doctors' timing	Time	Minutes
		Process control	Checks per line item	Number
2	All questions answered	Operator training	Training time	Hours of training
		Training process effectiveness	Testing	Passing grade
		Insurance knowledge	Training time	Hours of training
3	Short time to schedule	Care available	Care types	Quantity of care types
		Doctor staff level	Number on staff	Quantity of doctors with skills
		Schedule flexibility	Scheduler and type of care	Ability to schedule type of care

Figure 7.16 The doctor's office customer design matrix log.

	Material	Material	Methods	Methods	Machine
	System	Friendliness	Knowledge	Able to help	Time to appointment
Appointment					

Figure 7.17 Beginning of the quality house.

house for the customer needs. Figure 7.17 is an example of what part of the quality house looks like as they begin to build it.

In order to verify that the appointment process performs well, they may have to run a study (experiment) with different experience or knowledge levels, and personalities of receptionists to determine if they greatly affect the time to make an appointment. The different people who work as receptionists in the office participate in the experiment.

The team establishes the methods and approach for the experimental design and the data to be collected. They need to select sample sizes, equipment, people to perform the experiment, and people to perform the test under controlled conditions. To evaluate the results they need to obtain results from observers or blind callers.

They need to consider how to select the sample of callers in order to eliminate any bias and conduct a fair evaluation. They repeat this test with customers of a competitive doctor's office using the same customer input to obtain the competitive analysis.

Once they have established the caller test, they then run further tests to verify system capability and capacity in the process. They use this measure (capacity) for controlling appointment timing. Consider the following possible causal factors:

- Personality
- Healthcare experience
- Training
- Experience in the doctor's office
- Process knowledge

They study these variables to obtain the optimum level for the receptionist. Through their experiments, they come up with the best selection for the five variables noted above. The design team creates the ultimate formula or recipe. Once it is in place, they control the recipe or the process. They eventually verify the sensitivity of the process to the five variables through an experiment, if they do not complete one during the design process. They must consider the design of experiments throughout the construction of the quality house. (See appendix B for the outline and use of designed experiments.) Figures 7.18 and 7.19 show this development of technical requirements.

To evaluate the scheduler performance they test input checks performed, the database for procedure timing, and the ability to plan the output. They screen each doctor's abilities and match them to the patient's needs at the time of the call to understand the diagnostic requirements before scheduling the appointment. They also determine the process controls to put in place to assure that they handle each patient properly and schedule appointments quickly and correctly.

	Schedule	Schedule	Doctors' training	Process control	Process control	Process control	Process control
	Training	Data accuracy	Diagnoses	CPU speed	Input accuracy	System capability	System training
Time to appointment							

Figure 7.18 The doctor's office example of customer needs to technical hows.

Technical requirements / Customer consequences	Weighting	System available	Care available	Scheduler speed	Doctor training	Doctor staff size	Scheduler accuracy	Scheduler flexibility	Doctor flexibility	System capability	Operator training	System speed	System accuracy		
Time to appointment	8														
Choice of days	9														
Choice of times	5														
Short time to schedule	9														
Criticalness of visit determined	10														
Appointment made without interruption	5														
Appointment time kept	8														
All questions answered	9														
Insurance claims processed	8														
Insurance coverage recognized	10														

Figure 7.19 Quality house with customer input and final requirements on the doctor's office call.

EXERCISES

1. For the wine cooler customer input listed below and the good tasting coffee described and listed in the exercise in chapter 3, complete the input to the left hand side of the quality house and insure that the weighting is determined for the customer. Refer back to the exercises in chapter 3 for the needed information.

   Wine cooler:

Consequences	Attributes
• High quality	• Carbonated
• Less filling	• Crisp
• Refreshing	• Expensive
• Consume less	• Attractive label
• Quenches thirst	• Curved bottle
• Feminine	• Low alcohol

2. Now, based on the type of brand selection information you choose from chapter 3 and the data developed from the first exercise, determine the required processes and parameters to meet the customers' needs or wants based on the consequences and attributes identified. Build the top of the quality house for the information to be developed.

ENDNOTES

1. Bradley T. Gale, *Managing Customer Value: Creating Quality and Service that Customers Can See* (New York: The Free Press, 1994).
2. Ronald G. Day, *Quality Function Deployment: Linking a Company with Its Customers* (Milwaukee: ASQC Quality Press, 1993).
3. Ibid.
4. Ibid.
5. Ibid.
6. Ibid.

Chapter 8

The Critical Relationships

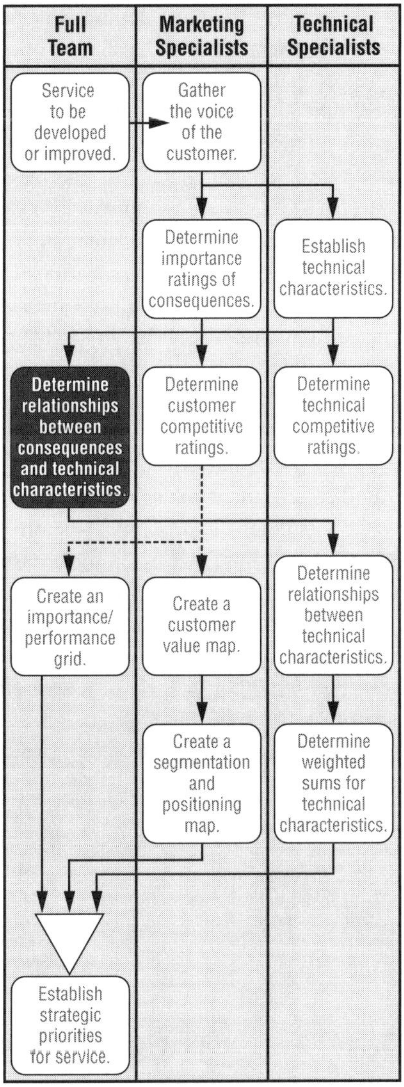

CHAPTER TOPICS

- Determination of Requirements
- Determination of Relationships between Consequences and Requirements
- Analyzing the Technical Matrix
- Development of Measurements
- Setting Optimal Levels
- Technical Competitive Analysis

CHAPTER TOOLS

- Cause-and-Effect Diagrams
- Brainstorming
- Customer Design Matrix Log
- Quality House

In chapter 7, we developed the technical hows, or requirements, and considered the relationships between the customer needs and the technical hows. When describing the voice of the customer analysis, we indicated the need to determine if the matrix had any potential problem areas by looking at the coverage of the relationships between the fundamental requirements for each consequence or need.

In this chapter, we complete the technical portion of the quality house. Figure 8.1 illustrates the flow of this process. We cover how the technical requirements relate to the whats and the desired level of each how. This part of the quality function deployment house lists and structures the technical requirements identified by the technical team. The technical hows are methods, company measures, design requirements, substitute quality characteristics, and engineering characteristics, which are related to the customers' needs.[1] This process provides a formal linkage between the objectives, or the customers' consequence, and the responses, or the hows. From the matrix, we provide a systematic method for developing or deploying the hows from the whats and for setting priorities.

After determining the relationships, the next task is to fill in the floor of the house with the required measures and values. Good hows must be measurable and affect the whats. To properly define the hows, each should be associated with a measurement unit and a direction. We determine the measurement units and the preferred direction of the measure for improvement for each technical requirement.

We determine through analysis how much (or the level) of the measured requirement to deliver to the customers to best satisfy their needs. To make this determination, we measure each how and its relationship in meeting the customers' needs. In most cases, this requires some testing of levels and ranges of the requirements, or hows.

Finally, we adopt improvement directions for each of the hows. The directions can be the more the better, the less the better, or a target best level, based upon which best satisfies the customers' needs. Figure 8.2 shows the flow of these steps.

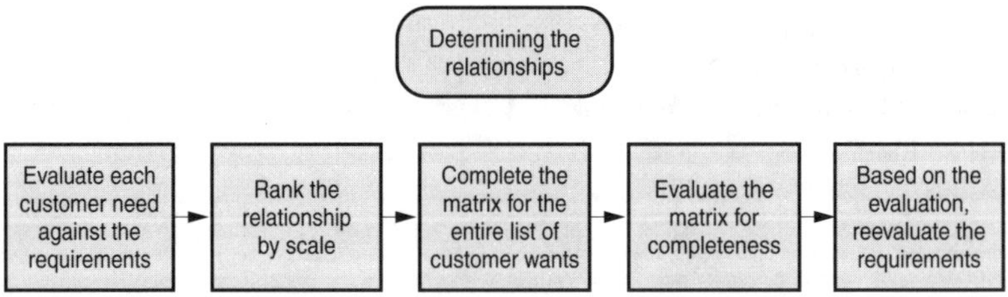

Figure 8.1 Flow of the concepts for this chapter.

Customers' voice	Technical requirements	Measurement units	Optimal value of the measure

Figure 8.2 Flow of steps.

One principle benefit of the QFD process is to allow people in the organization to guide the process development in the right direction. The technical portion of the quality house is a convenient place to deposit all the information we collect through this process, as we illustrate in this chapter. Any member of the organization can refer back to this portion of the house to recall the technical requirements, optimal levels, and directions of improvement.

DETERMINATION OF REQUIREMENTS

Let us review the pizza delivery example from chapter 7. Figure 8.3 shows the customer consequences with the weightings assigned by the customers, with one being lowest and 10 being highest.

We used the customer design matrix log that Figure 8.4 shows to list the design concepts that came from the customer's voice and provide detailed design considerations. The log provides a base for reference as we progress through the conceptual design phases.

We brainstormed cause-and-effect diagrams to develop the technical requirements. We may not easily be able to connect an important customer requirement with any valid and appropriate technical requirement. If the team does not accurately articulate how to meet a customer requirement, the final service process is unlikely to satisfy customers.

We write the requirements to meet the customer consequences across the top, or ceiling, of the quality house. Figure 8.5 shows part of the quality house with the technical requirements in place.

DETERMINATION OF RELATIONSHIPS BETWEEN CONSEQUENCES AND REQUIREMENTS

After we establish the customer consequences and technical requirements, we determine the relationships between them. The determination of these relationships helps with prioritization of the technical requirements (hows) and the decision of which ones are critical in the design of our service processes.

Technical requirements / Customer consequences	Weighting												
Sauce covers dough	4												
Cut all the way through	3												
Generous toppings	8												
Generous cheese	8												
Many choices of toppings	4												
Not greasy	10												
Sauce not watery	5												
Distinct sauce flavor	9												
Largo topping pieces	7												
Not all dough	9												
Done all the way	10												
Uniform pieces	3												
Does not droop when picked up	6												
Fast delivery	9												
Pizza hot	8												
Good every time	10												
Choice of types	6												
Not stuck to box	8												

Figure 8.3 The quality house with the customer's weighted input.

No.	Customers' Voice	Technical Requirements	Measuring Units	Value
1	Quick delivery	Drop-off points	Location	Direct
		Air	Planes	Direct
		Ground	Trucks	Direct
2	Low cost	Shipping alternatives	Dollars	Direct

Figure 8.4 Customer design matrix log.

Technical requirements / Customer consequences	Weighting	Retain heat of pizza	Hot temperature	Baking process	Timely delivery	Knowledge of area	Process capacity	Fresh toppings	Packging type	Order many toppings	Order process
Sauce covers dough	4										
Cut all the way through	3										
Generous toppings	8										
Generous cheese	8										
Many choices of toppings	4										
Not greasy	10										
Sauce not watery	5										
Distinct sauce flavor	9										
Large topping pieces	7										
Not all dough	9										
Done all the way	10										
Uniform pieces	3										
Does not droop when picked up	6										
Fast delivery	9										
Pizza hot	8										
Good every time	10										
Choice of types	6										
Not stuck to box	8										

Figure 8.5 The quality house for pizza delivery with technical requirements.

Although we created each how to measure one particular what, some of the hows are related to more than one what, as Figure 8.6 illustrates. We use a matrix to untangle the web of relationships between whats and hows. We indicate both where relationships exist and the strength of these relationships, as Figure 8.7 shows.

The scale used to indicate the relationships between the hows and the whats is somewhat subjective. We usually consider these scores as a ratio of the different relationships. These scores or weights are key to the determination of the critical hows or requirements to carry forward for further development in other rooms of the quality house. The scores also link the actual service process in the final room to its effects on the customers.[2]

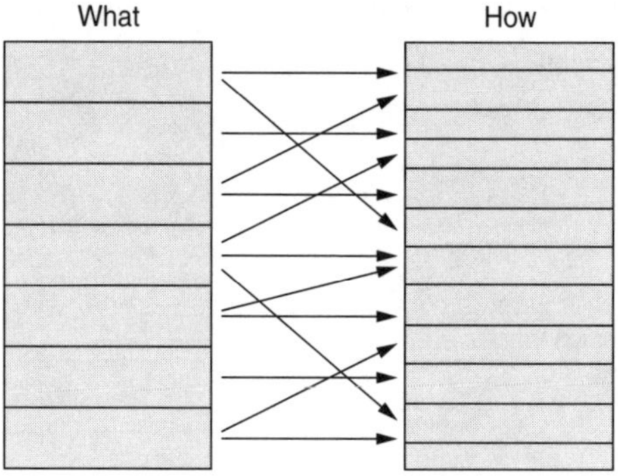

Figure 8.6 Some hows affect more than one what.

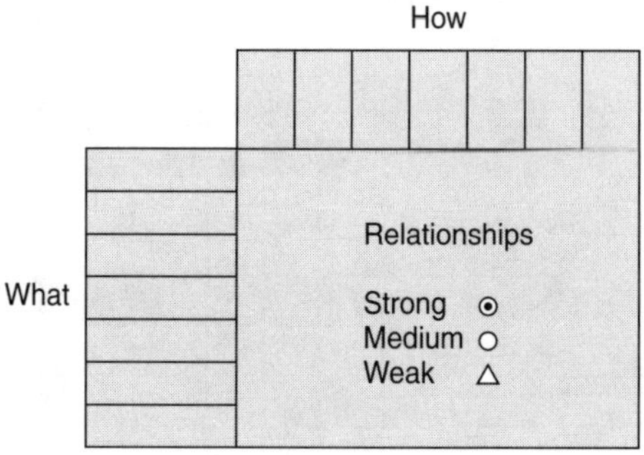

Figure 8.7 Untangling the web.

The symbols we use are common to the matrix analysis in the house of quality and we use them to indicate the team's evaluation of the relative degree of linkage, if one exists, between the customer consequence and the technical how. If a relationship exists, then the team needs to decide if it is relatively small (a weighting of one), medium (a weighting of three), or strong (a weighting of nine). As can be seen by these weightings, we correlate the values to the relationship strength. Stronger relationships have bigger impacts on meeting customers' needs and on the importance of the feature or function we are considering in the matrix analysis.[3]

The relationship matrix of the customer whats versus the technical hows is a systematic means for identifying the degree of the relationship or linkage between each consequence/what and each how/technical requirement. Filling in the matrix relationship for a column, we start with a how and determine which customer consequences it affects. The team compares each how to every consequence or what.

Let us look at the pizza example again. The values we use for the relationships (blank if no relationship exists) are high or major, medium, or minor by using the symbols ⊙, ○, △ respectively. We weight these as nine, three, and one, respectively. We use these weights later to establish which requirements we must support to satisfy customers.

A blank row or column indicates no relationship. A triangle △ indicates a small relationship exists which is valued as one (1). A circle ○ indicates a medium relationship exists which is valued as three (3). We indicate a high relationship with a double circle ⊙, which is valued as nine (9). We fill in the relationships for the pizza example consequences and requirements that were determined above. The partial completed house in Figure 8.8 shows the values for the relationships for the pizza example. Note that Figure 8.8 does not show all consequences or requirements due to space limitations.

Technical requirements / Customer consequences	Weighting	Retain heat of pizza	Hot temperature	Baking process	Timely delivery	Knowledge of area	Process capacity	Fresh toppings	Packaging type	Offer many toppings	Order process	Sauce preparation	Cutting process	Meat types	Cheese types
Sauce covers dough	4											△			
Cut all the way through	3												⊙		
Generous toppings	8														
Generous cheese	8														
Many choices of toppings	4									⊙				○	
Not greasy	10														⊙
Sauce not watery	5											⊙			
Distinct sauce flavor	9											⊙			
Large topping pieces	7												⊙		
Not all dough	9											△			
Done all the way	10			⊙	⊙										
Uniform pieces	3												⊙		
Does not droop when picked up	6			⊙	⊙										
Fast delivery	9				⊙	⊙					○				
Pizza hot	8	⊙	⊙	○	⊙				⊙						
Good every time	10							⊙						⊙	⊙
Choice of types	6									⊙				○	
Not stuck to box	8			○					○						○

Figure 8.8 The quality house for delivered pizza with relationships.

ANALYZING THE TECHNICAL MATRIX

A rule of thumb is to have the ratio of technical requirements to customer consequences be between one and three. We should observe no pattern of the relationship indicators in the matrix. Some additional precautions are:

- If less than 30 percent of the cells in the matrix is filled, some desired consequences may not have adequate coverage by technical requirements. Lack of customer satisfaction may result.

- If more than 60 percent of the cells are filled with indicators of relationships, we may have listed too many technical requirements for the customer consequences. Having too many technical requirements leads to difficulty designing the service process and overly expensive services.

- If the symbols are grouped together in small groups and are not scattered throughout the matrix, it may indicate that we have not considered the relationships of the requirements with all the consequences. Note that you will see some grouping if you place the requirements in the ceiling in the order of the consequences to which they were originally associated.

All these indicators show that potential problems exist with our choices of the technical hows, or the thoroughness of our analysis of the relationships.

DEVELOPMENT OF MEASURES

Once we have identified all the technical requirements and the matrix is completed, we check that we have a means of measuring each requirement. If measures are missing, we develop them or reconsider the requirement that we defined for the related consequence. Figure 8.9 shows how we

	Sorting process	Shipping method	Delivery method	Package handling	Package type				
Low-cost delivery									
	Time to process	Time and cost	Time and cost	Amount of damage	Amount of damage				

Figure 8.9 The delivery process with technical requirements for cost of delivery.

might link some measurements to the technical requirements for cost of the delivery process.

SETTING OPTIMAL LEVELS

Now our task becomes more difficult since we must select the optimum level and best direction for the measures. Is a lower or higher or target value desired for the result to better meet the customer's requirements? The answer to this question will help us develop the true requirements that will satisfy the customer's needs. Some examples to consider in the process of deciding the final value and direction of the requirement are[4]:

Bigger is better	Smaller is better
Heavier is better	Lighter is better
More is better	Less is better
Faster is better	Slower is better
Longer is better	Shorter is better
Brighter is better	Darker is better
Meeting the target is better	Missing the target is better

One way of approaching this task would be to consider the optimal value as the requirement is determined. We look at the same requirements we did in chapter 7 for customer service needs and add the optimal values for the requirement. Figure 8.10 shows how we might have considered these for the pizza delivery example.

Quick response	______	Time to respond (10 seconds max.)
	______	Time to complete transaction (5 seconds)
	______	Time to deliver (20 minutes max.)
Clean facility	______	Cleanliness standard (Best)
Hot pizza	______	Core bags (temperature change in 20 minutes)
	______	Speedy delivery (10 minutes)
	______	Cook at location (close to house)
	______	Cook on way (equipment type)

Figure 8.10 Examples of requirements with optimal values added.

Customer consequences \ Technical requirements	Ship air	Ship ground	Sorting process	Costs of process	Cycle time process
Delivered overnight	⊙		⊙	⊙	⊙
Day I want it	○		○	○	○
Within budget		○	⊙	⊙	⊙
No damage	○	⊙	⊙	⊙	⊙
Value	10 hrs	24 hrs	5 hrs	$2.00	10 to 24 hrs

Figure 8.11 The shipping process example of the completed matrix.

Figure 8.11 shows an example of setting the optimal values or levels for a package delivery example and where they are placed in the quality house.

Once we have developed the ranges of the measures, the next step is to indicate if it is better to hit a target value or to be higher or lower in value. Sometimes, we need to experiment with the output requirements of the process to make this decision. This may require the use of designed experiments to satisfy the customer consequences. Figure 8.12 again shows the quality house for pizza delivery, this time with the measures, directions, and optimal values added. The symbols used for this example are: increasing value = ↑, decreasing value = ↓, and target value = ○.[5]

TECHNICAL COMPETITIVE ANALYSIS

Now we have completed the matrix, ceiling, and floor of the first room of the quality house. (We completed the left side in chapter 5 and the right side in chapter 6.) Next, the team completes a competitive analysis on the technical requirements, including our capability to meet them.

In chapter 6, we used a questionnaire to conduct a customer competitive analysis on the customers' desired consequences. We select the same competitors to use here in the technical competitive analysis. Two major differences are: (1) that this analysis is completed against the technical requirements rather than the desired consequences, and (2) this analysis is an objective look at our capabilities and those of the competition, rather than a subjective assessment by customers.

Customer consequences \ Technical requirements	Weighting	Retain heat of pizza	Hot temperature	Baking process	Timely delivery	Knowledge of area	Process capacity	Fresh toppings	Packaging type	Offer many toppings	Order process	Sauce preparation	Cutting process	Meat types	Cheese types
Sauce covers dough	4											△			
Cut all the way through	3												⊙		
Generous toppings	8														
Generous cheese	8														
Many choices of toppings	4									⊙				○	
Not greasy	10														⊙
Sauce not watery	5											⊙			
Distinct sauce flavor	9											⊙			
Large topping pieces	7												⊙		
Not all dough	9											△			
Done all the way	10			⊙	⊙										
Uniform pieces	3												⊙		
Does not droop when picked up	6			⊙	⊙										
Fast delivery	9				⊙	⊙					○				
Pizza hot	8	⊙	⊙	○	⊙				⊙						
Good every time	10							⊙						⊙	⊙
Choice of types	6									⊙				○	
Not stuck to box	8			○					○						○
Direction		↑	○	○	↓	↑	↑	○	○	↑	↓	○	↓	↑	↑
Value		250°F	350°F	275°F	30 maximum	Map	Quantity	Date	Type	Number	2 minutes	Mix receipt	Minimum size	Five types	Five types

Figure 8.12 The quality house for delivered pizza with measures, directions, and values.

The design team evaluates the technical competitive analysis against the key requirements to determine how our product or service actually compares to the alternatives or competitors. The next chapter covers the technical competitive assessment.

THE DOCTOR'S OFFICE

The staff of the doctor's office developed the technical requirements, as we saw in chapter 7. Before determining the relationships between the whats and the hows, the team discussed how the customer makes a decision about which doctor to go to and whether the support functions of the office affect the choice of doctor. During this process, they developed a flowchart for a call to the office, as shown in Figure 8.13.

Once they had developed the flowchart, they looked at what variables might affect the call process flow. Using brainstorming and a cause-and-effect diagram, they created a table of the major factors, shown in Figure 8.14.

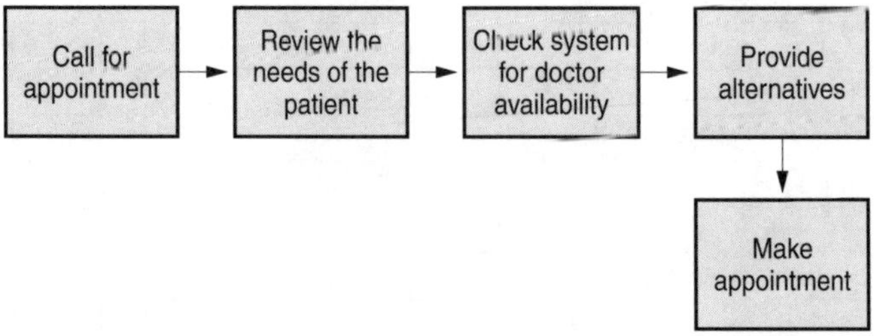

Figure 8.13 Process flowchart for doctor's office call.

	Machine	People	Material	Methods	Machine
	System	Friendliness	Knowledge	Able to help	Time to appointment
Appointment	⊙	△	○	⊙	⊙

Symbols: None = No relationship
△ = Minor relationship
○ = Medium relationship
⊙ = Major relationship

Figure 8.14 Technical information matrix for making an appointment at the doctor's office.

Next, the staff studied the relationships between each how, as they are developed from the information matrix, and every what. They met as a group to complete this analysis of relationships. Figure 8.15 shows one what with the hows that might affect it. The team came to a consensus on the strength of these relationships.

Once they had completely enumerated the relationships, they started looking at the measures and optimal levels of the technical hows. Figure 8.16 shows the addition of the measurement goals to the partial matrix given in Figure 8.15. Figure 8.17 shows the final matrix with the relationships indicated.

	Scheduler	Scheduler	Doctor training	Process control	Process control	Process control	Process control
	Training	Data accuracy	Diagnoses	CPU speed	Input accuracy	System capability	System training
No waiting time in office	⊙	○	○	△	△	△	○

Figure 8.15 The doctor's office example of relationships between customer consequences and technical requirements.

	Scheduler	Scheduler	Doctor training	Process control	Process control	Process control	Process control
	Training	Data accuracy	Diagnoses	CPU speed	Input accuracy	System capability	System training
No waiting time in office	⊙	○	○	△	△	△	○
How much	Effective-ness	100%	Skill number	10u sec.	100%	Input checks	Effective-ness

Figure 8.16 Example of the doctor's office correlation with the measures selected.

Customer consequences \ Technical requirements	Weighting	System available	Care available	Scheduler speed	Doctor training	Doctor quantity	Scheduler accuracy	Scheduler flexibility	Doctor flexibility	System capability	Operator training	System speed	System accuracy
Time to appointment	8	△	○			◉	◉	○	◉	◉	◉		○
Choice of days	9		◉		◉	◉	◉	◉	◉				○
Choice of times	5		◉		◉	◉	◉	◉	◉				○
Short time to schedule	9			◉			◉			◉	○	◉	○
Criticalness of visit determined	10								○		◉		
Appointment made without interruption	5	○		◉		△	○			◉	◉	○	○
Appointment time kept	8					◉		△	○		○		
All questions answered	9				◉						◉		
Insurance claims processed	8	○								◉	◉		
Insurance coverage recognized	10		○			◉							
Value		↓	↑	↑	↑	↑	↓	10 sec.	↑	↑	↑	↓	↑
How much		System downtime in hours	Number of caregivers	1000 MHz processor	Trained in necessary care	Number of doctors available	Software errors	Software capacity	Doctor care training	Number of software featueres	Training effectiveness	System response of 1 second	Software capability

Figure 8.17 The doctor's office call with the matrix completed with requirements, measures, and relationships.

The doctor's office example shows the correlation between the customers' desired consequences and the processes that the doctor's office has to use to fulfill the consequences. As you can see from the matrix, the office team feels that scheduler accuracy based on software will have the biggest impact on reducing the waiting time in the office when a patient arrives for an appointment. This is just the first step in evaluating each customer consequence against the process that currently is in place to fulfill it. If the team develops key processes to meet each of the customer consequences, then all the consequences from the left side of the house will tie to a process in the matrix. The next chapter discusses this in more detail.

EXERCISES

1. Develop the technical requirements and measures for the wine cooler consequences in problem number one of chapter 7 and good tasting coffee for the house selected and started in chapter 7 from data in chapter 3.

2. After you develop the requirements and measures, fill in the relationship matrix for the customer consequences and the technical requirements for the wine cooler consequences in problem one of chapter 7 and the coffee house.

ENDNOTES

1. Eve Burke, Jack M. Kloeber, Jr., and Richard F. Dekro, "Using and Abusing QFD Scores," *Quality Engineering Journal* 15, no. 1 (2002–03).
2. Ibid.
3. Chan Lai-Kow and Ming-Lu Wu. "Quality Function Deployment: A Comprehensive Review of Its Concepts and Methods," *Quality Engineering Journal* 15, no. 1 (2002–03).
4. Ibid.
5. Ibid.

Chapter 9

Technical Competitive Analysis

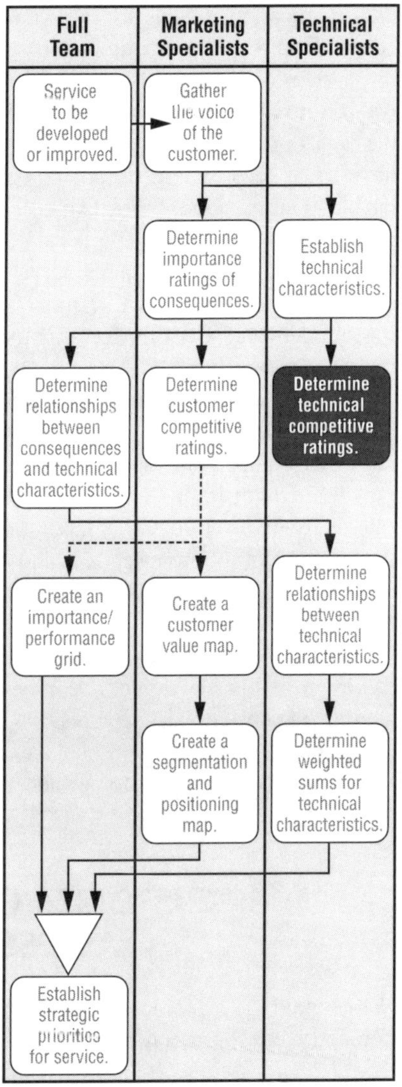

CHAPTER TOPICS

- Customer Competitive Assessment
- Technical Competitive Assessment
- Comparing the Competitive Analyses
- Marketing and Sales Analysis

CHAPTER TOOLS

- Mystery Shopper
- Observation
- Sales Point
- Experimental Design

In this chapter, we cover how to compare our performance with that of the competition. Customers do not evaluate our service in a vacuum, separate from the services of competitors. They evaluate all service providers to purchase the one that offers them the greatest value. For a restaurant, customers will compare the service not only to what they expect from that restaurant, but also to the service provided by other restaurants of the same type.

If we are to capture a share of the customer's business, we need to understand how our services compare to those of our competitors. Knowing the organizations' strengths and weaknesses on all aspects of a service in comparison to the competitors is essential for the organization to improve its services and competitiveness. If we are developing a new service, then we need to discover how our potential customers are meeting their needs at the present time. Even if we offer a unique service, our customers probably have some other means of getting service to meet their needs, unless we have a total monopoly. For example, we may offer an internal computer purchasing service to all employees of our company. Unless the company forces all employees to use our service, a number may make computer purchases on their own. If we want to get them to use our services, then we must understand why they feel that they get a better value from making the purchase themselves.

We can perform competitive comparisons in a number of ways. We can have customers rate our performance and that of known competitors. This customer competitive assessment will give us the customers' perceptions, which is reality in the marketplace. Alternatively, we can have customers rate alternative services in a laboratory setting. Usually, we provide them descriptions of different services and ask the customers to rate them. In this situation, we generally avoid letting customers know who provides each of the services described.

We can also evaluate our services and those of our competitors ourselves, a technical competitive assessment. Sometimes we use publicly available materials, such as brochures, to obtain information on the services of our competitors. Other times, we may use a mystery shopper, a person who plays the role of customer and evaluates the services provided by us and by our competitors.

CUSTOMER COMPETITIVE ASSESSMENT

We covered the customer competitive assessment in chapter 6. We use the competitive information obtained through that process in the development of the quality function deployment house to determine in what areas customers perceive that we are not performing as well as the competition. This knowledge helps us find opportunities to improve on our service performance. The design team uses this information to improve on key features or requirements of the service process performance. The customer competitive analysis portion of the planning matrix is the repository for the quantitative data we obtain.

TECHNICAL COMPETITIVE ANALYSIS

The customers' perceptions of the competition comes from service evaluations performed by the customers themselves.[1] The technical evaluation of the competition and the service we provide come from the engineering and technical staff that design the service process to be offered to the customers. They may set up tests of the competitive services, evaluate existing information about competitive services, or develop evaluation forms that mystery shoppers complete. Another alternative is to observe customers actually using each of the services.

The results of whatever method you use are stored at the bottom of the quality house and used to evaluate your service against the alternatives. As for the customer competitive analysis, the alternatives may not come from your known competition. These comparative evaluations will lead to establishing strategic goals for the service process to better satisfy customers' needs.

We may also develop sales points to indicate the organization's competitive position and opportunities. We compute the final ranking of the order of the customer's needs and strategic importance from the competitive and customers' needs input analysis. This provides the whys of the process to indicate why we should work on the whats through the competitive evaluations of the whats, strategic goals and the sales points assigned to the whats, and strategic importance derived for the whats.

Figure 9.1 gives an example of the results of a customer competitive analysis on customer consequences and a technical competitive analysis on the technical requirements of alternative package delivery services.

We can improve on our performance by evaluating how the technical requirements can be designed, controlled, and fine-tuned to become more consistent and to exceed both competitors' performance and customers' needs and expectations. When customers rate our performance on a consequence as less than optimal, we review how the competition compares to us on the related technical requirements. We use this comparison to evaluate how we can adjust the technical requirements to meet or exceed customers' needs and expectations.

		Auto sort	Air ship	Surface delivery	Hand carry	Hand sort	Hand delivery					1 2 3 4 5
Fast delivery												X □ O
Cost of delivery												X□O
No damage												O□X
Value		1 sec.	1 day	3 days	5 days	2 hours	5 days					
Technical analysis	1	X	X	O	□							
	2			X	O	□						
	3	□	O			O	X					
	4			□			□					
	5	O	□		X	X	O					

X = Our delivery □ = Best competitor O = Next competitor

Figure 9.1 Competitive analysis for a delivery process.

The development or engineering team that is part of the service design department performs the technical comparisons. For each feature or process requirement, the technical team measures our service and the service of the competition, or alternatives to our service that the customer is using today.

We must perform the technical evaluation at least on those competitors that the customers noted during the interviews or focus groups that were part of the voice-of-the-customer analysis. You may feel other comparisons that were not identified by the customers should be made, and then you add them to the technical evaluation.

The testing performed is actually observing and using the service. A mystery shopper may visit your competitors, playing the role of a customer. The mystery shopper evaluates all competitors on the most objective measures that you can create. The technical evaluation focuses on the values of the technical requirements that are critical to fulfilling customers' needs. This testing can be time-consuming, but it is worthwhile to assure that your service will be competitive and valued by customers.

In this step in the quality house, we need to perform specific tests on the service output or performance versus the requirements of the process. This requires a carefully planned test process using your own personnel with specified inputs and uses for the process or service. Under controlled conditions or testing routines, we monitor the specified output or performance to determine the results compared to the customers needs and their perception of those needs being filled. This can lead to specific experiments to determine key process factors that affect the output.

The tests will require good collection methods for the data and the data analysis. The knowledge must be obtained on how the data will be used to determine performance and how the analysis of the data will take place. This will help to determine how to proceed with the data collection process. This can lead to the development of data collection sheets or check sheets and specified test methods to follow to better control the data collection process. The data collection process must consider the analysis process since this could bias our collection methods process. The sample size we take and the sample's representativeness of the population we are studying also are critical. This applies to all data collection processes.

The technical verification of key requirements by the design team will help us understand the level of performance needed to satisfy the customers' needs. This may lead to further process, service, or product analysis to verify the customers' needs against the requirement parameters.

Let us look at a package delivery example to see what the results of the technical evaluation look like. We start with some givens:

- The customer wants a package delivered on time.
- We can provide a variety of alternative shipping methods based on costs.
- We can control the sorting, shipping, and selection process developed to help with the product delivery.

Figure 9.2 covers how the cost of delivery might look.

COMPARING THE COMPETITIVE ANALYSES

We now compare the results of the technical evaluation on the bottom of the QFD house to the customers' competitive evaluation on the consequences. For example, we compare the customers' evaluation of the cost of delivery, which rates USPS lower in cost than UPS, with the technical analysis that rates USPS higher based on actual fee rates. When such a disagreement occurs, then the marketing and sales staff address the discrepancy with communications to the customers. The sales force needs to overcome the disadvantage that the customer perceives in order to make the sale.

Figure 9.3 shows how we compare the customer competitive analysis and the technical competitive analysis for pizza using two adjacent columns.

		Sorting process	Shipping method	Delivery method	Package handling	Package type	Competitive analysis 1 2 3 4 5
Delivery cost		⊙	⊙	⊙	○		X □○
Value		1 day	Air/ surface	Hand air	Auto hand	Soft hard	
Technical evaluation	1	X	□	○	X	□	
	2	□	X		○		
	3		○	X		○	
	4	○		□	□	X	
	5						

X = USPS □ = UPS ○ = FedEx

Figure 9.2 Technical requirements for the customer needs of the delivered package.

	Weighting		Weighting	Technical requirements	Measuring units	Competitive technical analysis Us = X A = □ B = ○ 1 2 3 4 5	Customer competitive analysis Us = X A = □ B = ○ 1 2 3 4 5
Tastes good	10	Sauce not watery	5	Sauce preparation	Recipe mix	○ X □	□X○
		Distinct sauce flavor	9	Sauce preparation	Same as above	○ □ X	X ○ □
		Large topping pieces	7	Fresh toppings: vegetable, meat, cheese	Age or pull date, and variety	X □ ○	□ ○X
		Not all dough	9	Same as above	Same as above	X□○	X○□
		Not greasy	10	Same as above	Same as above	□○X	□○X

Figure 9.3 Customer needs and technical requirements for a good tasting pizza.

Using this approach shows the comparison of the technical evaluation that the team performed on actual pizza delivery service to the customers' input on the competitive service. Any discrepancies indicate areas that we must study further to decide on our approach to resolving them.

MARKETING AND SALES ANALYSIS

Marketing and sales determine approaches to improve customer satisfaction. They determine areas to concentrate on in advertising and sales processes, and approaches to these areas. Often, they find the approach evident after they compare the two competitive assessments. Any discrepancies that exist are an indication of a market need. Marketing and sales are critical to this process since they communicate with the customer and the market. Major issues in the marketing strategy and advertising campaigns come from this process.

Once we know the organization's and the competitors' performance on each customer consequence, the next step is to establish goals for each consequence. These goals are numerical and are consistently based on the competitive rating scale used in the customer competitive analysis. For example, the pizza delivery organization may want to improve from a rating of three to a rating of four on "not greasy."

We also determine sales points for consequences on which we excel. A sales point highlights the organization's ability to provide the desired consequences better than anyone else. We should provide strong sales points for the higher-weighted consequences. We may not create sales points for less important consequences since they do not have as much impact on the customers' buying decisions for our service.[2]

Figure 9.4 shows the customer competitive analysis and the technical competitive analysis for the pizza delivery example.

THE DOCTOR'S OFFICE

The doctor's office example shows the customers' competitive perceptions and the staff's technical evaluation. The staff collected the customers' perceptions with a questionnaire, as we described in chapter 6. They then evaluated their own performance on the technical requirements. For the competition, they evaluated their own experiences at other doctors' offices on the technical requirements.

This process of technical evaluation is very time-consuming and sometimes is skipped because of the costs and time involved. The service industry

Technical requirements / Customer consequences	Weighting	Retain heat of pizza	Hot temperature	Baking process	Timely delivery	Knowledge of area	Process capacity	Fresh toppings	Packaging type	Offer many toppings	Order process	Sauce preparation	Cutting process	Meat types	Cheese types	Competitive analysis Us = X A = □ B = ○ 1 2 3 4 5
Sauce covers dough	4											⊙		△	△	X ○□
Cut all the way through	3												⊙	△	△	□○X
Generous toppings	8							○		△		○		⊙	⊙	X○□
Generous cheese	8							⊙							⊙	□ X○
Many choices of toppings	4							△		⊙		○		⊙	⊙	X○□
Not greasy	10													⊙	⊙	□○X
Sauce not watery	5							△				⊙		⊙	○	□X○
Distinct sauce flavor	9											⊙		○	○	X○ □
Large topping pieces	7							⊙		○				⊙	⊙	□ ○X
Not all dough	9											⊙		⊙	⊙	X○□
Done all the way	10		△				○				△			⊙	⊙	□ ○ X
Uniform pieces	3												⊙	○	○	○□ X
Does not droop when picked up	6											△	○	○	○	□ X○
Fast delivery	9	△	△		⊙	⊙	○		△		⊙		△	△	△	□○X
Pizza hot	8	○	⊙			○	△		⊙		○			△	△	○ X□
Good every time	10	△	△				△	⊙	△	○		⊙		⊙	⊙	○□ X
Choice of types	6						△	○		⊙		⊙		⊙	⊙	X □○
Not stuck to box	8								○				○		⊙	○ □X
Value		↑ 250°F	○ 275°F	○ 350°F	↓ 30 mins.	↑ Map	↑ Quantity	○ Date	○ Type	↑ Number	↓ 2 mins.	○ Mix receipt	↓ Minimum size	↑ Five types	↑ Five types	
Technical evaluation same symbols	1	□	○		○		□		○	□	X		X	□	X	
	2	X		□	X		○		X						□	
	3	○		X	□	□	X	X	□		□	□	○		○	
	4		X	○		○		□		○	○	○	□	○		
	5		□			X		○		X		X		X		

Figure 9.4 The pizza quality house.

Customer consequences \ Technical requirements	Weighting	System available	Care available	Scheduler speed	Doctor training	Doctor staff size	Scheduler accuracy	Scheduler flexibility	Doctor flexibility	System capability	Operator training	System speed	Training process	Screening process	Insurance knowledge	Competitive analysis
Time to appointment	8	⊙	⊙	⊙		⊙	⊙	⊙	⊙	⊙						X ○ □
Choice of days	9	⊙	⊙		⊙	⊙	⊙	⊙	⊙	⊙						○ X □
Choice of times	5	△	⊙		⊙	⊙	⊙	⊙	⊙	⊙						X ○ □
Short time to schedule	9	⊙	⊙		⊙	⊙	⊙	⊙	⊙	⊙		⊙				□ ○ X
Criticalness of visit determined	10										⊙		⊙	⊙		X ○ □
Appointment made without interruption	5	⊙	⊙	○			⊙	⊙	⊙	⊙	⊙	⊙		⊙		○ X □
Appointment time kept	8	△			○	⊙	⊙	△	⊙	⊙	⊙			⊙		□ X ○
All questions answered	9										⊙		⊙		△	○ X □
Insurance claims processed	8	○									⊙		⊙		⊙	X ○ □
Insurance coverage recognized	10										△		⊙	⊙	⊙	□ X ○
Column weight																○ X □
Value		↑	↑	↑	↑	↑	↑	↑	↑	↑	↑	↑	○	○	↑	
Measure		1	1	1	3	3	3	1	1	3	3	1	1	1		
Technical analysis same symbols	1	○	□		□	X		X	□	X	□		□	X	□	
	2				○	○		○		○	○		○			
	3	X	X	○	X	□	□	□	○		X	X	X	○	X	
	4	□	○	X			○			□		○			○	
	5			□			X		X			□		□		

Measure code: 1 = Faster speed 3 = More is better

Symbol: X = Us ○ = Office 1 □ = Office 2

Figure 9.5 Doctor's office process specifications example.

needs to become more familiar with this step and use the comparisons to evaluate the organization's own performance against the competition on the technical requirements of the service process.

At this stage of the evaluation, the team compares the customers' evaluations to the actual test results for the office and the team's evaluation of other offices.

The office scored higher than office 1 but lower than office 2 on system availability. They evaluated this rating against how the customers perceive the office and competitive offices on consequences that are highly

	Competitive assessment	Difference
	1 2 3 4 5	
System available	O X □	
Time to appointment	X O □	Below
Choice of days	O X □	Same
Choice of times	X O □	Below
Appointment made without interruption	O X □	Same

X = Our office □ = Office 1 O = Office 2

Figure 9.6 Matrix of customer and technical evaluation comparisons.

related with system availability. The relevant consequences are: time to make an appointment, choice of days, time to schedule, and appointment made without interruption. They completed a small matrix, as shown in Figure 9.6, to look at these comparisons.

As they evaluated these areas, they saw that the office needs to improve on the time it takes to make the appointment and the choice of appointment times available. In both of these areas, the office is weakest in the customers' perceptions. The team rated themselves as better than office 2, but the customers did not agree. On the other two relevant consequences, customers considered the office to be better than office 2 but behind office 1. In these areas, the team evaluates why the office is behind office 1. Since system availability does seem to be influencing these important consequences, the team will develop a strategy to improve the office process for system availability. The team continues to evaluate each technical requirement in a similar manner.

The *relationship matrix,* as the central part of the matrix is sometimes called, systematically identifies the degree of relationship between the wants and the hows. The customers' perception of the organization's performance to that of the competition[3] helps the staff understand the customers' needs and how well the organization is meeting those needs today. The design team can develop a plan to assure the new process will exceed the needs and provide a competitive advantage. The staff may promote the resulting sales feature in its *Yellow Pages* advertising and via other means.

Even without advertising, customers will note the office's better performance and be delighted. For example, if they can provide a rapid, error-free office scheduling system that allows quick, accurate appointments for the patient, then the patients will all notice the difference when they next schedule an appointment. The matrix allows the staff to intelligently evaluate such concepts as online appointment scheduling and automated phone answering.

EXERCISES

1. In performing a competitive analysis, customer input is required for the comparison to be made. Define the various methods that you can use to obtain the competitive analysis. Then select the different types of questions that you would use to obtain the information.
2. What are some of the actions that can be taken when the analysis shows that the competition is better at meeting the needs of the customer than the organization is?
3. Perform the competitive analysis for the shipping process based on your own experiences.

ENDNOTES

1. Ronald G. Day, *Quality Function Deployment: Linking a Company with Its Customers* (Milwaukee: ASQC Quality Press, 1993).
2. Lai-Kow Chan and Ming-Lu Wu, "Quality Function Deployment: A Comprehensive Review of Its Concepts and Methods," *Quality Engineering Journal* 15, no. 1 (2002–03).
3. Ibid.

Chapter 10

Technical Correlations and Trade-offs

CHAPTER TOPICS

- Technical Correlations for the Roof of the Quality House

CHAPTER TOOLS

- Relationship Diagrams
- Brainstorming
- Block Diagrams
- Designed experiments

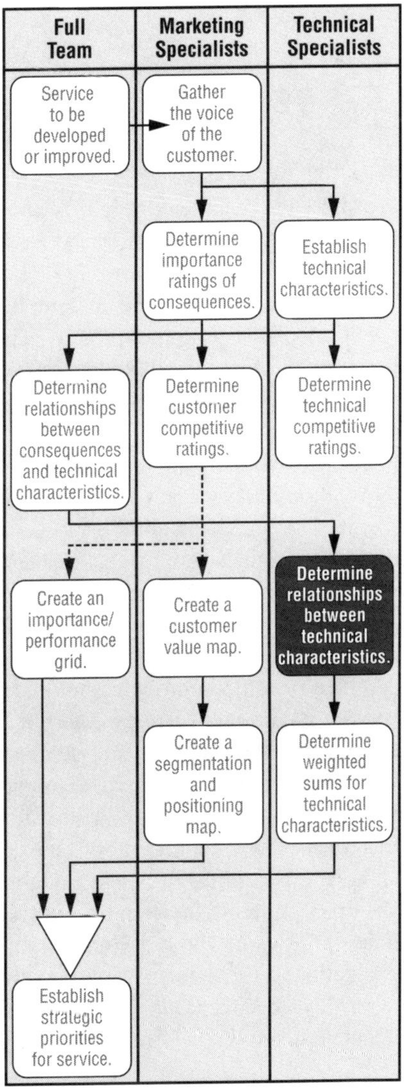

The design process puts together the key block diagram and design concepts for the service you provide to the customer and marketplace. This process helps us in the analysis of trade-offs between the technical requirements. We use the roof of the quality house to show the design requirements correlations between each set of two requirements. Each pair will have no correlation, a positive correlation, or a negative correlation between them. The design team develops the correlations using brainstorming or designed experiments when the team cannot readily determine the correlations. In this chapter, we establish the roof of the quality house.

TECHNICAL CORRELATIONS FOR THE ROOF OF THE QUALITY HOUSE

We show the technical trade-offs at the roof of the house for the technical requirements chosen to meet the customer needs. Here we are looking for positive, negative, or no correlation between the technical requirements that we established to meet the customers' desired consequences as defined by the voice-of-the-customer process. The roof is sometimes difficult to establish because we may not know the relationships or we might not be able to verify them. If this is the case, we will have to conduct further testing and correlation analysis for the variables (the technical requirements). The testing may be some form of comparison testing or designed experiments. The correlation analysis helps us establish good design parameters, which are required to meet customer's needs and expectations. Since the process design specialists (engineers) provide the technical requirements to meet the customer consequences, they also determine the relationships or correlations that exist between each pair of requirements. This team leads the process for filling in the roof of the quality house.

The development team should see how one requirement might affect another requirement as they determine the hows for the technical portion of the matrix. The direction and degree of the correlations between the technical requirements have serious impacts if one how affecting the other represents design difficulties. Those hows that are related negatively with respect to others represent bottlenecks in the design that will call for special planning or design breakthroughs to solve the conflict.

In completing the technical correlation matrix or roof, the team establishes tests using the requirements that affect the activity or function it is evaluating. The tests may require the development of an experiment to determine the interaction of the requirements on the output responses or dependent variables. Statistics and research design books develop the experiments we use. We have provided some simple points to consider and further references in appendix B.

The roof of the quality house (this may be why we call this matrix a house) quickly becomes the group's design control method to assure that we consider the interactions between the technical process parameters. These interactions will affect the customers' needs if we are not careful. The measures we established for these items are used now to our advantage to design the process so the interactions have the least amount of impact on the final process and, in turn, we will provide for the customers' desired consequences.

Testing approaches to consider for determining the correlations between technical requirements are:

- Laboratory prototype evaluation
- Simulated operational performance
- Alpha test sites to evaluate performance
- Past experiences and test data

Now we take the pizza example and apply this approach to determine the correlation between the requirements we use to develop the pizza delivery process. Determining the relationships between the technical requirements is important when we develop the approaches used to create the consequences for our customers. The process team reviews all the correlations that can exist by checking each possible pair of requirements. The correlation symbols used for the roof are:

Correlation:	
High Positive	★
Low Positive	×
Low Negative	⊙
High Negative	○

Figure 10.1 shows a correlation matrix for the pizza example for your review and analysis.

We have filled in most of the roof correlations for the analysis of the pizza. Some other considerations may surface as we proceed to analyze the affects of the technical features that are associated with ordering, preparing, baking, and delivering the pizza. This correlation analysis is important to the design of the processes that will allow us to deliver quality pizza on-time to meet various customers' needs. The trade-offs made here will be

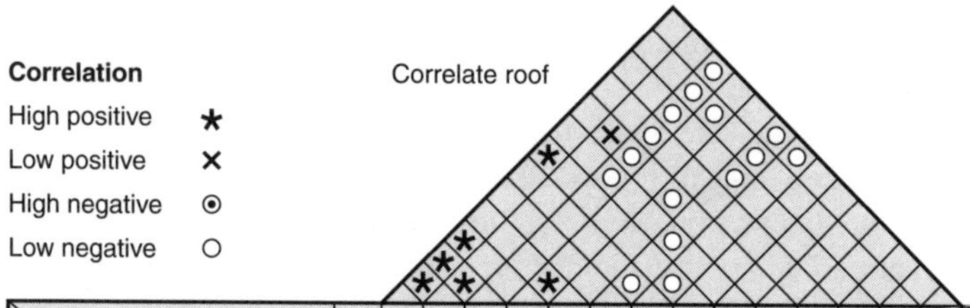

Customer consequences \ Technical requirements	Weighting	Retain heat of pizza	Hot temperature	Baking process	Timely delivery	Knowledge of area	Process capacity	Fresh toppings	Packaging type	Offer many toppings	Order process	Sauce preparation	Cutting process	Meat types	Cheese types	Competitive analysis Us = X A = □ B = ○ 1 2 3 4 5
Sauce covers dough	4											⊙		△	△	X ○□
Cut all the way through	3												⊙	△	△	□○X
Generous toppings	8							○		△		○		⊙	⊙	X○ □
Generous cheese	8							⊙							⊙	□ X○
Many choices of toppings	4							△		⊙		○		⊙	⊙	X○□
Not greasy	10													⊙	⊙	□○X
Sauce not watery	5			⊙				△				⊙		⊙	○	□X○
Distinct sauce flavor	9											⊙		○	○	X○ □
Large topping pieces	7							⊙		○				⊙	⊙	□ ○X
Not all dough	9											⊙		⊙	⊙	X○□
Done all the way	10		△	⊙			○				△			⊙	⊙	□ ○ X
Uniform pieces	3												⊙	○	○	○□ X
Does not droop when picked up	6			○								△	○	○	○	□ X○
Fast delivery	9	△	△		⊙	⊙	○		△		⊙		△	△	△	□○X
Pizza hot	8	○	⊙	⊙		○	△		⊙		○			△	△	○ X□
Good every time	10	△	△	⊙			△	⊙	△	○		⊙		⊙	⊙	○□ X
Choice of types	6						△	○		⊙		⊙		⊙	⊙	X □○
Not stuck to box	8								○				○		⊙	○ □X
Values		↑	○	○	↓	↑	↑	○	○	↑	↓	○	↓	↑	↑	

Figure 10.1 A portion of the finished pizza quality house.

important to meeting customers' needs and the ability to deliver a service that will exceed what is available from the competition at the time.[1] The technical process owners and delivery personnel conduct this correlation analysis to be sure we have covered all necessary relationships between the technical requirements.

Delivered overnight	______	Ship air (time)
	______	Ship ground (time)
	______	Sort for location (time)
Day I want it	______	Same (air)
	______	Special sort by day (time)
	______	Two or more days (ground)
Within budget	______	Shipping type cost
	______	Sort costs (time)
	______	Cycle time costs
No damage	______	Package design
	______	Shipping method
	______	Cycle time

Figure 10.2 Matrix development for shipping.

Let us now look at the shipping example. Figure 10.2 shows the matrix development approach for the shipping.

Note some of the high negative correlations identified in Figure 10.3. If the development team sets a low cycle time, then shipment by air will be required and costs will increase. These requirements represent significant trade-offs in the design.

Some items you want to consider during the process of developing correlations for the roof of the house are:

- Evaluate the response changes for each of the key parameters as the technical function or feature is related to the other technical feature or functions.
- The best way to verify the correlation is through testing each paired requirement and using a scatter diagram on one feature to the output of the other feature.
- A technical team is best at performing the correlation analysis. Experts in technical design, process design, materials, and customer contact personnel and manufacturing personnel should complete the roof of the house as a team.
- Negative correlations will present concerns for the process, function, or feature. Consider the trade-offs that you make when you change the value of either requirement.

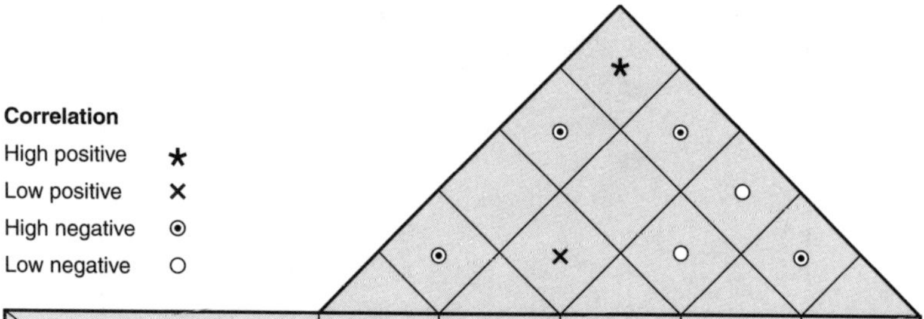

Technical requirements / Customer consequences	Ship air	Ship ground	Sorting process	Costs of process	Cycle time of process
Value					
Delivered overnight	⊙		⊙	⊙	⊙
Day I want it	○		○	○	○
Within budget		○	⊙	⊙	⊙
No damage	○	⊙	⊙	⊙	⊙
Value	10 hrs	24 hrs	5 hrs	$2.00	10 to 24 hrs

Figure 10.3 A portion of the shipping process quality house.

We have not seen many teams that build a quality house use this portion of the process effectively due to the difficulty in recognizing the correlations and the natural reluctance to conduct the tests required to identify and verify the correlations. Completing this stage is very important because many of the technical requirements in the final design may cause interference with the process performance because the team did not recognize critical interactions during the development phase. We should conduct designed experiments to verify the interactions before we proceed with the design so that we are sure about the interactions. Years of experience with product design have shown that awareness of correlations is very helpful in selecting proper levels of technical requirements to maximize performance of the service or product.

THE DOCTOR'S OFFICE

The staff of the doctor's office met as a team to consider the correlations between each pair of technical requirements. Figure 10.4 shows the correlations they hypothesized at their meeting. Even thought they felt confident about the direction of the correlations, the team recognized a need to study some of the relationships further.

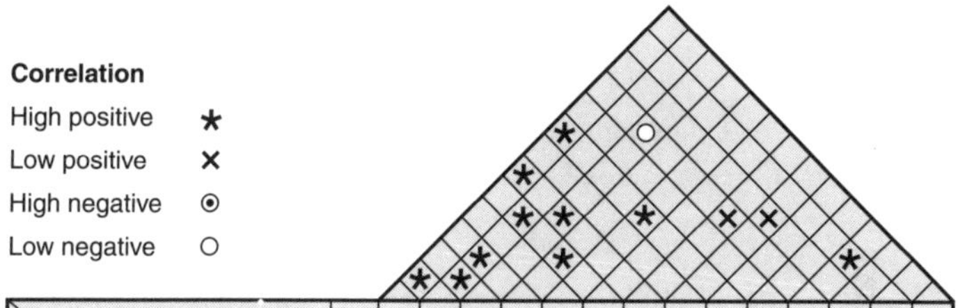

Customer consequences \ Technical requirements	Weighting	System available	Care available	Scheduler speed	Doctor training	Doctor staff size	Scheduler accuracy	Scheduler flexibility	Doctor flexibility	System capability	Operator training	System speed	Training process	Screening process	Insurance knowledge
Time to appointment	8	⊙	⊙	⊙		⊙	⊙	⊙	⊙	⊙					
Choice of days	9	⊙	⊙		⊙	⊙	⊙	⊙	⊙	⊙					
Choice of times	5	△	⊙		⊙	⊙	⊙	⊙	⊙	⊙					
Short time to schedule	9	⊙	⊙		⊙	⊙	⊙	⊙	⊙	⊙		⊙			
Criticalness of visit determined	10										⊙		⊙	⊙	
Appointment made without interruption	5	⊙	⊙	○			⊙	⊙	⊙	⊙	⊙	⊙		⊙	
Appointment time kept	8	△			○	⊙	⊙	△	⊙	⊙	⊙			⊙	
All questions answered	9										⊙		⊙		△
Insurance claims processed	8	○									⊙		⊙		⊙
Insurance coverage recognized	10										△		⊙	⊙	⊙
Value		↓	↑	↑	↑	↑	↓	10 sec.	↑	↑	↑	↓	↑		

Figure 10.4 A portion of the finished doctor's office quality house.

EXERCISES

1. Using the data obtained for the weather resistant product in Figure 7.9 on weather effects, develop the technical requirements, the measures to be used, and the values.
2. Using the results of exercise one above, establish the correlation matrix for the roof of the house.

ENDNOTE

1. Ronald G. Day, *Quality Function Deployment; Linking a Company with Its Customers* (Milwaukee: ASQC Quality Press, 1993).

Chapter 11

Other Items to Consider in the Quality House

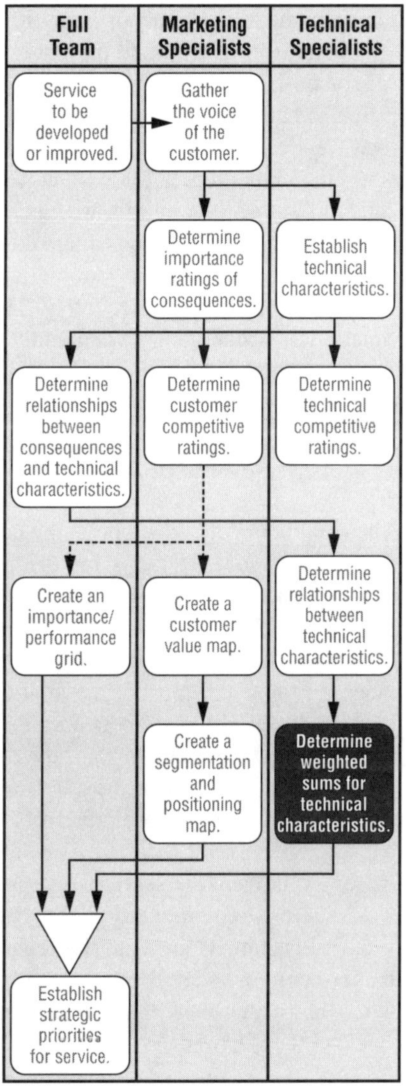

CHAPTER TOPICS

- Customer Complaint Column
- Priority Column
- Direction of Improvement
- Sales Improvement Column
- Relative Importance of Technical Requirements
- Customer Matrix

CHAPTER TOOLS

- Quality House
- Pugh Concept Analysis
- Conceptual Block Diagrams
- Customer Matrix

This chapter covers other voices that can enter the quality house. When customer contact people enter the needs for the process or product performance, they also develop the other customer voices. Then the team calculates the total column weights to decide the most critical requirements to take forward as the output of the first quality house. We add a column for recording customers' comments on services or complaints about problems. The complaints column is added as a column just before the customer competitive ratings. We correlate these comments with the competitive analysis that we performed in the last chapter. We use the customer competitive analysis and the importance weightings to evaluate which areas to concentrate on marketing and evaluating through customer satisfaction surveys. When we find a consequence that our organization provides better than the competition and which is important to customers, then we are in a position of strength. Sales and marketing will exploit this strength in communication with customers. If we find a gap requiring us to catch up to the competition, we can consider or reconsider new features or functions to provide a gain in this area.

Sometimes we find a customer consequence that we and other companies are not providing adequately. This gives us an opening to consider a function or feature that we can add to our process that will meet or exceed the customers' needs and expectations.

CUSTOMER COMPLAINT COLUMN

The complaint column supports the need for us to take charge and do something about specific areas requiring attention. This process allows the matrix to become more credible in the customer competitive analysis.[1] If you refer back to the Kano model presented in chapter 4, we want to select features or functions of our process that satisfy customers' desired consequences, those that do not dissatisfy customers' basic consequences, and those that delight customers through delivering their excitement consequences. Service features that are dissatisfiers are those that make customers dissatisfied when they are not present but do not provide any real satisfaction when they are present. An example would be the delivery of a package to the right location. The satisfiers are the functions that the customers want from the service process and usually will ask for. An example would be next-day delivery. For satisfiers, the more we provide, the more satisfied customers are with the organization's service. Lastly, the features that are delighters are those that will make customers pleasantly surprised when they occur but will not make them dissatisfied if they are not provided

Technical requirements / Customer consequences	Weighting	Retain heat	Hot pizza	Keep hot	Timely delivery	Knowledge of area	Capacity	**Complaints**
Direction of improvement		↑	○	↑	↑	↑	↑	
Sauce covers dough	4							20
Cut all the way through	3							37
Generous toppings	8							10
Generous cheese	8							0
Many choices of toppings	4							20
Not greasy	10							1
		250°F	350°F	275°F	30 min.	Map	Quantity	

Figure 11.1 Pizza delivery process example with complaint column.

because customers did not expect them. An example might be receiving an e-mail informing you that they delivered the package. The QFD process usually does not identify the delighters unless the design team makes a special effort to consider what they might be and provide added functions, attributes, or features of the service to deliver them.

We may want to create a separate matrix to compare the customer issues that we develop with the existing processes that are in place today. Figure 11.1 is an example of how this works on the pizza delivery process and product.

PRIORITY COLUMN

We may use this matrix with the added columns to help select priority issues that must be addressed by engineering, marketing, and sales. We take the customer weight of each consequence and multiply this times the number of complaints related to that consequence. We base the need for improvement of each consequence on the multiple of the number of complaints to the customer importance weighting. We may also calculate a ratio of the number of complaints to the customers' perceived level of our performance against the competition. The customer-weighted input for this new column allows the organization to consider the strength of the needs of the customers in making decisions on the importance of an area for improvement in the process. We not only want to exceed customers' expectations, we also want to resolve complaints presently noted about the service.

This new customer complaint column is only used to help decide which customer consequences must be addressed first for the process and the organization to be successful in the future.[2] We show examples of these calculations below. We place the results in a priority column within the quality house matrix as shown in Figure 11.2.

Example of the priority issues calculation:

Sauce covers dough = 4 × 20 ÷ (20 ÷ 4) or 80 ÷ 5 = 16

Example of the ratio using the complaint level to customer performance evaluation:

2 (goal) ÷ 3 (customer evaluation) = 2/3.

Technical requirements / Customer consequences	Weighting	Retain heat	Hot pizza	Keep hot	Timely delivery	Knowledge of area	Capacity	**Improvement goal**	Complaints	**Priority**	**Level of performance**
Direction of improvement		↑	○	↑	↓	↑	↑				
Sauce covers dough	4							2	20	16	3
Cut all the way through	3							1	37	9	
Generous toppings	8							4	10	67	
Generous cheese	8							4	0	0	
Many choices of toppings	4							2	20	16	
Not greasy	10							5	1	50	
		250°F	350°F	275°F	30 min.	Map	Quantity				

Figure 11.2 Pizza example with complaints, improvement goals, and priorities.

If customers perceive the organization as poor and the competition as better in meeting a consequence, then the organization must study the competition and note why they are better in meeting the specific needs of the customer (benchmarking). On consequences that customers perceive the organization to be superior in meeting, the organization must promote its superiority in its advertising and sales messages. On consequences where consumers consider us equal to the competition, we must find ways to improve the features or requirements that lead to providing the desired consequence to gain on the competition. We will consider the weighting of the specific consequences in the prioritization of the areas to focus on. We can deal with these concepts within the quality house or as a separate matrix used to provide sales and marketing guidance. The goal is to develop priorities for the improvement to be effective and meaningful to the customers.

DIRECTION OF IMPROVEMENT

We use the quality house to transform the voice of the customer into technical requirements that the organization can address in the design of the process or product. As an addition to the matrix, we take the function or feature from the ceiling of the house and define a measure that will be transformed into a formal specification for the process or product parameters that we must focus on to assure customer satisfaction with our service.

The analysis of the relationships between customer consequences and technical requirements helps determine the target values for the technical requirements. We use the how analysis to establish the optimum oven temperature and the length of time to bake the pizza to meet the customer consequences of melted cheese, cooked topping varieties, baked dough, and crispy crust. We may need to analyze two to three parameters in a well-designed experiment to discover the optimum settings for the technical requirements. The team discusses the consequences involved, the customers' importance ratings of the consequences, and our perceived performance in providing those consequences. The engineering group performs an analysis of our current values or parameters on the technical requirements and determines how we are performing against the consequences. They also select the target values for the requirements.

Once we know the targets of the measured requirements, we can establish whether a higher or lower value is better. The team then can plan for the action necessary to meet the requirements. The action taken must consider whether we need to improve to catch up with the competition, we should maintain our present level, or we have an opportunity to gain on the competition. While we are performing this analysis, we must also consider the roof of the house—whether the technical requirements have a negative, positive, or no relationship with each other. This will help determine the optimal level for the technical requirements.[3]

We measure the technical feature or requirement as part of the development of the technical hows. We then use the performance measures to specify the inputs required as standards to the process. Below are the symbols we use to indicate the target directions for the hows.

Symbol	Meaning
○	Meeting a definite target is better
↑	Bigger, faster, heavier, more, or longer is better
↓	Smaller, shorter, lighter, slower, or less is better
○↑	Target is best but higher is better than lower
○↓	Target is best but lower is better than higher

Another way to accomplish the task of identifying the levels and types of measures to achieve the requirement is to look at the customer consequence and determine how it will be met and, then, how much is needed. Let us look at this concept through the use of the cause-and-effect method. Figures 11.3 through 11.5 show examples of using this method to determine the direction of improvement for various technical requirements for pizza.

We use the quality house as a planning document for the improvement of the technical specifications we use in the process. As with the voice of the customer, we use the technical matrix for the development of technical specifications. Our job is to assure that we tie the customers' needs to the correct technical specifications or requirements during the conceptual phase of design and development. The next example shows how we develop good technical specifications into the design and development process for pizza.

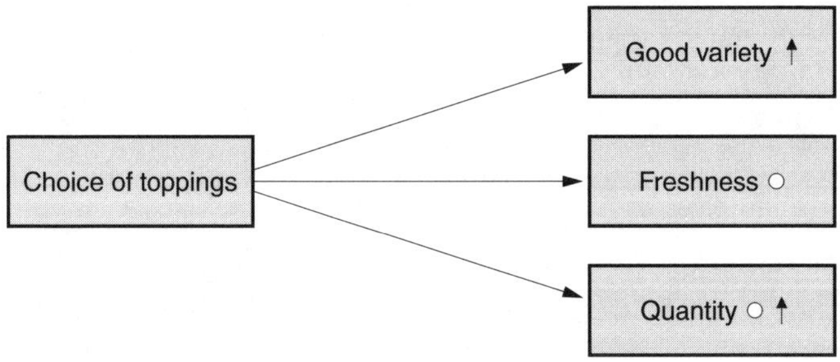

Figure 11.3 Cause-and-effect method for pizza toppings.

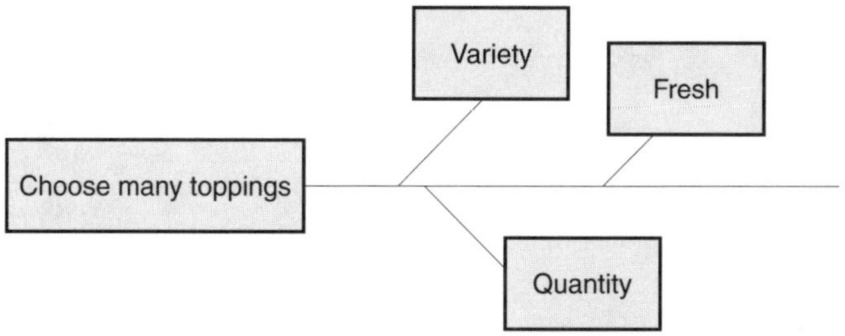

Figure 11.4 Cause-and-effect method for pizza toppings.

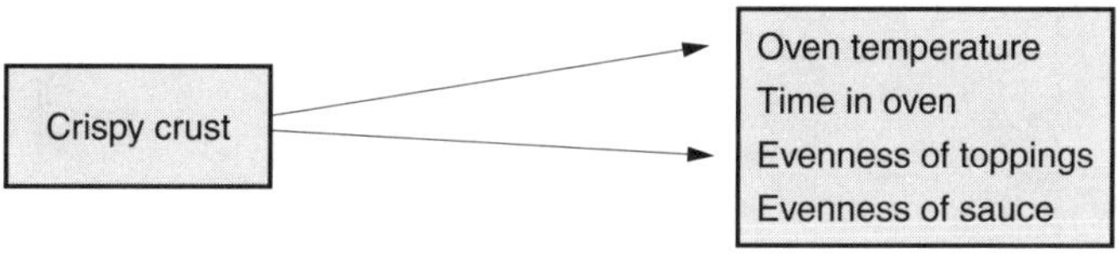

Figure 11.5 Cause-and-effect method for crispy crust.

As we analyze the technical matrix of the quality house, we must consider the following:

1. The matrix analysis should show how we integrate the customer needs into the technical requirements for the design and processes.
2. We should address all customer needs in a market niche.
3. All requirements, or hows, should contribute to delivering customer consequences.
4. About 60 percent of the relationships in the matrix should be full.
5. From the matrix analysis, we must decide on the goals to achieve customer satisfaction with the important consequences.
6. The analysis should provide a means to prioritize our efforts (requirements) in satisfying customers.
7. From the matrix analysis, we will determine which technical requirements we must work on and how to prioritize our efforts.
8. We tie the target values for the technical requirements to the process that affects the requirement and the controls that we have to put in place to maintain the process at those values.

Customer consequences \ Technical requirements	Weighting	Retain heat	Hot pizza	Baking process	Timely delivery	Knowledge of area	Packaging	Design inupts	Complaints
Direction of improvement		↑ B&E	○ A	○ D	↓ E	↑ E	↑ C	See A–C and D–E	
Sauce covers dough	4								20
Cut all the way through	3								37
Generous toppings	8								10
Generous cheese	8								0
Many choices of toppings	4								20
Not greasy	10								1
		250°F	350°F	275°F	30 minimum	Map	Type		

A–C: The recipe will define the bake temperature and bake time. The package material and type will keep it hot. The shipping container will maintain the heat.

D—E: The delivery time will depend on the driver's knowledge of the area (covered by training) and the transportation type of the driver (controlled during hiring).

The bake temperature, time in oven, packaging, and carrying device must keep and maintain the temperature of product.

Figure 11.6 Pizza technical specifications construction.

THE SALES IMPROVEMENT COLUMN

To establish our priorities for the organization, we can add some more information to the customer portion of the matrix. Once we tie the complaints and customer competitive evaluations to customers' assigned importance of the consequence, we can develop goals for sales improvements.

We need to weight the goals developed from the customer portion of the matrix on some scale (1 to 5 or 1 to 10) with the highest rating being the most important consequence to fulfill or provide. We review the sales improvement column to determine areas that we need to emphasize. We calculate a ratio of improvement needed by dividing the goal by the customer competitive evaluation. We rate both the customer competitive evaluation and the goal on the same scale (1 to 5 or 1 to 10) before we calculate this ratio. This improvement ratio shows which areas to prioritize for improvement. Sometimes organizations also calculate a weight column for the customer consequences. We multiply the customer importance rating by the improvement ratio and the sales goal for the values in this column. We use a scale of one, three, or nine to rate the sales goal column the same way we rated the internal matrix. The team provides action goals for those consequences that they weighted higher. The goals will relate to the customers' perceptions of our capability as compared to that of the competition. These action plans allow us to allocate our resources to areas that will improve customer satisfaction most.

The customer priorities lead to technical priorities, which become part of the conceptual design process. The team develops conceptual block diagrams as the beginning of the design process. Before we establish the conceptual diagrams, let's look at a tool that will help with the design process, the Pugh analysis, developed by Stuart Pugh.[4] It helps us select the critical items for the design. The steps for this analysis are:

1. Obtain the criteria for the design from the customer wants, needs, consequences, and expectations.
2. Include functions or features that will enhance the customer criteria.
3. Develop a group of design concepts that will satisfy the customer criteria.
4. Use a matrix to list the criteria and concepts for correlation.
5. Select one of the concepts as a datum against which to compare all other concepts.
6. Evaluate each concept against the datum as better (+) or worse (–).
7. Record the team's decisions.
8. For each column, determine the total number of pluses, minuses, and equals.

9. Improve the concepts that are the best.
10. Continue the process of synthesizing the concepts until the best one surfaces.

Figure 11.7 shows an example of the Pugh concept. The pluses and minuses in the matrix refer to the standard pizza that presently satisfies the customers. The processes then add to or subtract from the standard. An S indicates that the process will not add nor subtract from the standard since the customer is already satisfied.

We will use the critical criteria from this process to develop the design concept proposal in block form for all the functions or features that must be developed or improved. For the technical developments, we consider balancing the requirements to the established targets. This could lead to further testing or trial runs of the process. We must develop checks and balances on the performance against the required target we established during the matrix development.

Figure 11.8 shows the concept block diagram for pizza developed from the Pugh analysis. Figure 11.9 shows the concept block diagram for a shipping process so you can compare the two diagrams.

Concepts	Oven design for the baking process	Recipe of the sauce and its tomato source	Availability of toppings
Requirements			
Musts:			
1. Temperature of pizza	+	S	–
2. Tastes good	+	+	+
3. Sauce not watery	+	+	+
4. Generous toppings	S	S	S
5. Done all the way	+	+	–
Wants:			
1. Distinct sauce flavor 9	S	+	–
2. Good every time 10	+	+	+
3. Not greasy 10	+	+	+
4. Fast delivery 9	–	S	–
Wants totals:	11	29	2

Figure 11.7 Pugh concept example.

The baking process has to be developed for different volumes	The preparation process must follow a recipe	The topping types and preparation with proper coverage is required	The packaging and carrying process will be defined	The transportation and mapping process for delivery is to be developed

Figure 11.8 Concept block diagram for the preparation, baking, and delivery processes for pizza.

The sorting process must be devised to handle the bar codes to determine destination	The process cycle will have to be determined for the shortest methods to the destination	The air shipping process and route selection to key destinations must be developed	The packaging and carrying process will be defined	The ground transportation methods and process for delivery is to be developed for air and ground shipments

Figure 11.9 Example of the concepts for the design of shipping processes.

RELATIVE IMPORTANCE OF TECHNICAL REQUIREMENTS

Before we finish with the first quality house and move on to other phases and houses, we need to determine which technical requirements to carry forward in our design. We base this decision on the relative importance of each technical requirement for the process. We can use several approaches to assigning relative importance ratings to the requirements.

The first approach is highly quantitative. We use the consequences/requirements matrix to develop an initial rank ordering of the technical requirements. This matrix contains the linkage between the importance of the consequences and the technical requirements. Looking at one requirement at a time, we multiply the value assigned to its relationship with a consequence (9, 3, 1, or 0) times the importance of that consequence. Then, we sum the values for all consequences for the requirement at which we are looking. Then we repeat this process of multiplying and adding for all the requirements. The sums of the multiples are placed in a row at the bottom of the quality house. Figure 11.10 shows the final quality house with these sums for the pizza example.

The final weights provide the relative importance rating of each how for this process. A final weight is a comprehensive measure indicating the degree to which the specific how is related to the consequences, or whats, of the customers.

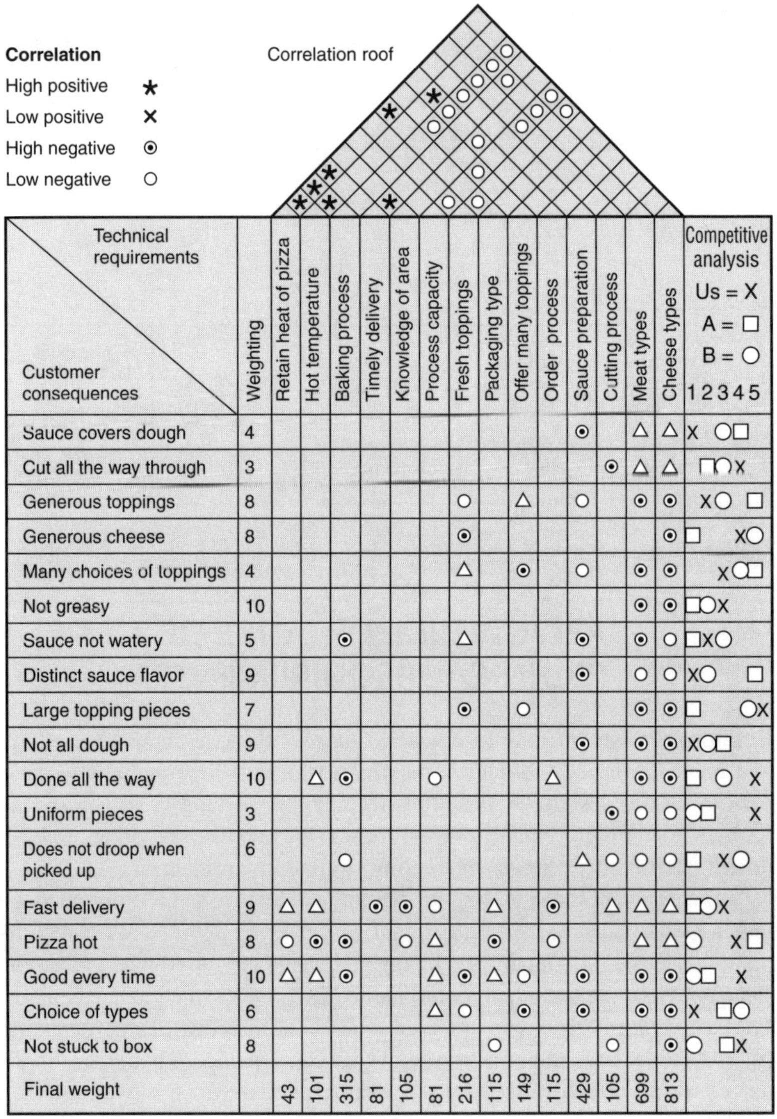

Figure 11.10 Finished pizza house.

The relative importance that we calculate determines each how's basic importance compared to the other hows. The technical how that receives the highest relative importance rating is most important to meeting the most important consequences, or whats, and creating satisfied and loyal customers.

	Weight by customer	Linen change process	Cleaning bath process	Room prep process	Carpet	Furniture	Lighting and TV
Bed made	9	⊙					
Clean bathroom	10		⊙	○			
Vacuumed	8		○	⊙	⊙		
Dusted	6			⊙		○	
Lighting	6			⊙			⊙
Coffee and etc.	4			⊙			
Weight		81	114	246	72	18	54

Figure 11.11 Made-up hotel room example.

The higher the relative importance, the greater the competitive priority of that how. The higher the gap between our performance on the technical requirement and that of the competition or the ideal, the greater the detriment to customer satisfaction. For the pizza example shown in Figure 11.10, the most important requirements are: cheese types, meat types, sauce preparation, and baking.

Look at two other examples of these calculations to get a better feel for what this analysis does for us. Figure 11.11 shows the final weights for making up a hotel room. For this partial example, room preparation process is most important, followed by cleaning bath process. We will spend most of our time in this phase of the quality function deployment developing these requirements.

Figure 11.12 shows a partial example for servicing a washing machine. Here, three requirements stand out in importance: diagnostic process, cycle time to travel, and cleanup process.

Another approach we can use to determine the relative importance of each technical requirement is an importance–performance grid, which we will describe more thoroughly in chapter 13. The team considers our performance on each requirement compared to our competition, the technical competitive assessment, and the performance dimension. The importance dimension comes from the final weights. The team selects those requirements that are high in importance and low in performance as its first priorities for further analysis.

For each how, the technical team could also determine the technical difficulty for the organization to meet the how much (target) for the defined

	Weight by customer	Service available	Parts available	Diagnostic process	Clean-up process	Cylcle time to travel	Cycle time to repair	Complaints	Priority
Cost	10					⊙	⊙	15	227
Service time	8	⊙	⊙	⊙	⊙	⊙	⊙	10	100
Time to deliver service	7	○	○			⊙		5	25
Cleanliness of service	5				⊙			2	4
Effectiveness of service	8			⊙				10	100
Weight		93	93	144	117	225	162		

Figure 11.12 Product service example for washing machine complaint.

how. We identify the target as high or low in difficulty to achieve. The team considers the level of difficulty along with the parameters given in the last paragraph. It may select less difficult requirements to tackle first. On the other hand, a high difficulty level indicates a need for a breakthrough analysis of the key process parameters to achieve the technical requirement. If we can establish a unique process to assure we provide the customers' consequences, we will have a strong competitive advantage.[5]

CUSTOMER MATRIX

Sometimes we want to match the requirements to specific customers when the customers vary widely in what they desire. We use this more frequently in business-to-business services where we have a small number of important customers. We set up a matrix that maps the requirements to the customers to determine which requirements have the highest priority for each customer. Figure 11.13 shows an example. The rows represent different customers or markets.

THE DOCTOR'S OFFICE

The staff of the doctor's office had kept a record of patient complaints over the prior year. The staff added these complaints to the quality house, as shown in Figure 11.14.

	Delivery time	Topping variety = 10	Bake process	Packaging	Crust thickness	Familiar with area	Complaints	Priority
Cincinnati		⊙	⊙	⊙	⊙	○	10	
Fort Mitchell	⊙	○		⊙	○	⊙	6	
Erlanger	⊙	⊙	△	⊙	○	⊙	9	
Edgewood	⊙	○	△	⊙	○	○	5	
Norwood	○	○		⊙	○		6	
Wilder		○	△	⊙	○		5	

Figure 11.13 Example matrix to match objectives to the customers.

Technical requirements / Customer consequences	Weighting	System available	Care available	Scheduler speed	Doctor training	Doctor staff size	Scheduler accuracy	Scheduler flexibility	Doctor flexibility	System capability	Operator training	System speed	Training process	Screening process	Complaints
Time to appointment	8	⊙	⊙	⊙		⊙	⊙	⊙	⊙	⊙					10
Choice of days	9	⊙	⊙		⊙	⊙	⊙	⊙	⊙	⊙					5
Choice of times	5	△	⊙		⊙	⊙	⊙	⊙	⊙	⊙					20
Short time to schedule	9	⊙	⊙		⊙	⊙	⊙	⊙	⊙	⊙		⊙			15
Criticalness of visit determined	10										⊙		⊙	⊙	3
Appointment made without interruption	5	⊙	⊙	○			⊙	⊙	⊙	⊙	⊙	⊙		⊙	4
Appointment time kept	8	△			○	⊙	⊙	△	⊙	⊙	⊙			⊙	5
All questions answered	9										⊙		⊙		3
Insurance claims processed	8	○									⊙		⊙		4
Insurance coverage recognized	10										△		⊙	⊙	7
Value		↓	↑	↑	↑	↑	↓	10 sec.	↑	↑	↑	↓	↑		

Figure 11.14 The doctor's office example with complaints.

EXERCISES

1. Take the doctor's appointment example from this chapter and calculate the priority for the key customer items.
2. For the doctor's appointment example, redefine the measured value and determine if you can develop better indicators.

ENDNOTES

1. Ronald G. Day, *Quality Function Deployment: Linking a Company with Its Customers* (Milwaukee: ASQC Quality Press, 1993).
2. Ibid.
3. Ibid.
4. Ibid.
5. Ibid.

Chapter 12

Matrices for Parts, Processes, and Supplier Needs

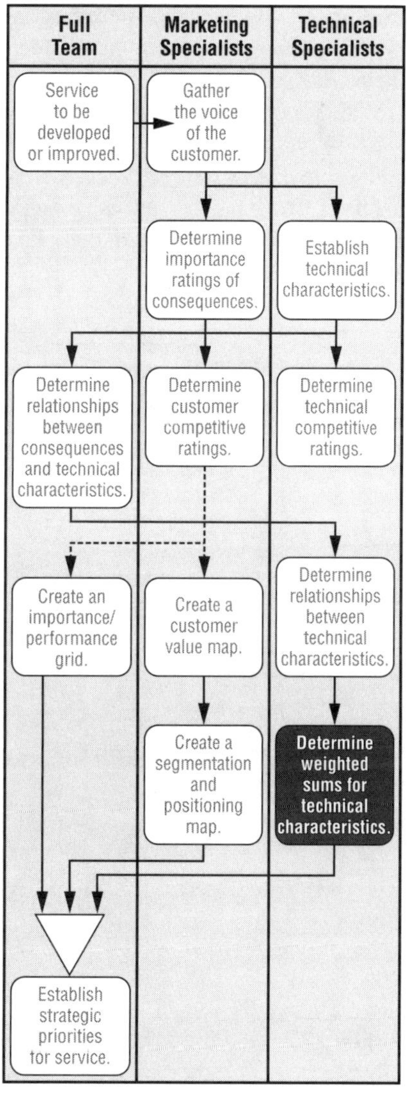

CHAPTER TOPICS

- Four Phases of QFD
- Process Specifications
- Parts Parameters

CHAPTER TOOLS

- Quality House
- What/How Matrices

In this chapter, we consider the deployment of the technical requirements into other houses or rooms at different levels. The input to the next room of the house comes from the output of the previous room. This output to input chain from room to room allows us to track the part, process, and supplier requirements back to the voice of the customer. The key point for service development is the linkage from the customer priorities to the parts specification, process controls, and supplier input requirements. We link the service customer to the key parameters of the process. From the key process parameters, we develop process controls to assure that we will provide the customer consequences. The key in service processes is to develop key characteristics or parameters that affect the output of the service process. Sometimes we have to test these parameters to verify that they actually control the process output and are key to performance.

We can look at the total quality function deployment house in several phases, levels, or rooms. Figure 12.1 shows each of these phases, beginning with the first quality house developed in chapters 7 through 11. Notice how the hows from the matrix in one phase become the whats for the matrix in the next phase.

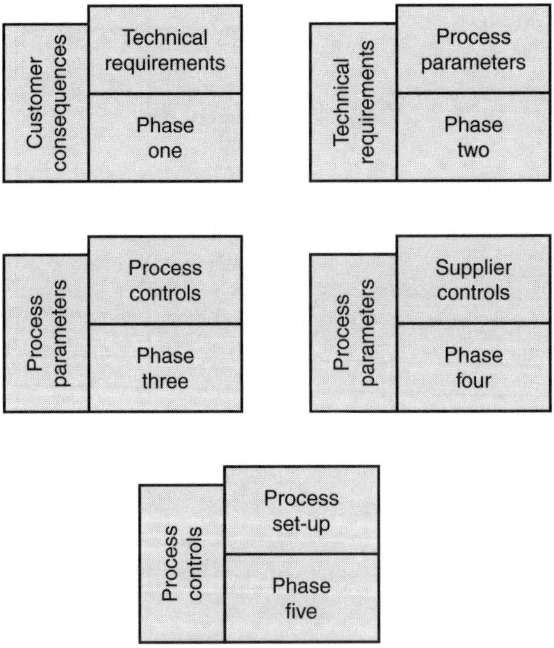

Figure 12.1 The five phases of quality function deployment.

The next four phases are:

- Develop key process characteristics or parts requirements
- Set up inputs to process controls
- Develop supplier requirements for the process
- Develop process setup parameters

Phase two is to generate process and/or part characteristics or parameters from the technical requirements brought forward from the planning matrix. From the parts characteristics, we set up key process controls required to produce a consistent process that meets the characteristics. We also use the process and part characteristics or parameters to determine supplier requirements. We may also develop process setup requirements from the process controls, such as a standardized layout in the processing area of a fast food restaurant. These setups help control the process for consistency. For services, the process is critical to consistent delivery of the service, something all customers want and expect.

PROCESS SPECIFICATIONS

The inputs to the next room or house come from the technical requirements, or hows, of the planning matrix. Each how, defined as a priority through using the final weights, is used as the input to the next phase. As the team prioritizes the needs in the first matrix, they assign people to phase two, determining the activities we will use to fulfill the process requirements.[1]

The design team transfers the requirements with high final weights from the hows of the planning matrix into the whats of the next house matrix. We provide an importance weight for the technical requirements by dividing the final weight by 10. This gives a priority weight to the whats of the process matrix or the parts matrix that corresponds to the importance rating we used for the customer consequences in phase one. The next step is to develop the process parameters or characteristics that we will establish with corresponding levels of performance to deliver the technical requirements. We must develop the service using the priority weights for the process requirements developed from the final weights of the first house.

We proceed with the development of the matrix in the same way we did in phase one. We will not include the customer competitive analysis or the technical competitive analysis in this matrix since we will be talking about our internal processes. Once we determine the strength of the relationships between the technical requirements and the process parameters, we then create the final weights for the parameters, which will provide the key parameters that we must control for our process or are critical for supplier delivery.

Figure 12.2 shows some of the translations of the key technical requirements and their values into process parameters that are required to deliver the pizza that meets the customer's desired consequences.

PARTS PARAMETERS

Figure 12.3 shows how we evaluate the critical requirements for parts necessary for the process against the input requirements for the technical

Technical requirements	Critical process specifications	Weight	Oven temperature	Baking time	Evenness of heat
Hot pizza	275°F	8	⦿	⦿	⦿
Baking	350°F	10	⦿	⦿	⦿
Timely delivery	30 minutes	9			○
	Process specifications		350 ±10°F	20 min. ±1	
	Column weight		170	170	251

Figure 12.2 Process parameter development for baking a pizza.

Technical requirements	Critical part specifications	Weight	Packaging	Topping selection
Hot pizza	275°F	8	⦿	○
Generous toppings	1 oz. each	8		⦿
Timely delivery	30 minutes	9		
	Process specifications		Seal PSI	Weight oz.
	Column weight		72	96

Figure 12.3 Part parameter development for preparing a pizza.

Technical requirements / Customer consequences	Weighting	Ship air	Ship ground	Sorting process	Costs of process	Cycle time process
Value						
Delivered overnight						
Day I want it						
Within budget						
No damage						
Value		10 hrs	24 hrs	5 hrs	$2.00	10 to 24 hrs
Direction		↓	↓	↓	↓	↓
Weight						

Figure 12.4 Shipping process example.

requirements. These parts may come from another internal process or from an external supplier.

Figure 12.4 provides an example for the package shipping service process. See if you can complete the evaluation and weighting based on your experience with this process.

With the use of the multiple phases of the QFD house, we link the entire organization to the customers' needs or desired consequences. A major benefit is that all parts of the process from set up through implementation now tie back to how they will affect the customers. Trade-offs can then be determined to optimize the entire process to fulfill the consequences of the customer. We deploy the customers' voice throughout the organization to assure a central focus on the customer. The QFD house is a formal, structured, and systematic way to transform the customers' desires for a service into prioritized technical requirements, process and parts parameters, process controls, process setup, and supplier controls.

THE DOCTOR'S OFFICE

The doctor's office example shows the entire process of taking the requirements from the initial planning matrix to the parts parameters for the office to deliver to the requirements of the key processes and supply the customers'

Customer consequences \ Technical requirements	Weight	System available	Care available	Scheduler speed	Doctor training	Doctor staff size	Scheduler accuracy	Scheduler flexibility	Doctor flexibility	System capability	Operator training	System speed	Training process	Screening process	Insurance knowledge
Time to appointment	8	⊙	⊙	⊙		⊙	⊙	⊙	⊙	⊙					
Choice of days	9	⊙	⊙		⊙	⊙	⊙	⊙	⊙	⊙					
Choice of times	5	△	⊙		⊙	⊙	⊙	⊙	⊙	⊙					
Short time to schedule	9	⊙	⊙		⊙	⊙	⊙	⊙	⊙	⊙		⊙			
Criticalness of visit determined	10										⊙		⊙	⊙	
Appointment made without interruption	5	⊙	⊙	○			⊙	⊙	⊙	⊙	⊙	⊙		⊙	
Appointment time kept	8	△			○	⊙	⊙	△	⊙	⊙	⊙			⊙	
All questions answered	9										⊙		⊙		△
Insurance claims processed	8	○									⊙		⊙		⊙
Insurance coverage recognized	10										△		⊙	⊙	⊙
Value		↑	↑	↑	↑	↑	↑	↑	↑	↑	↑	↑	○	○	↑
Final weight		268	324	86	215	351	396	332	396	396	370	126	333	297	171

Figure 12.5 Doctor's office technical requirements.

desired consequences. Figure 12.5 shows the original doctor's office example from chapter 7 with a few additions.

From Figure 12.5, the staff took forward the highest priority technical requirements. Figure 12.6 illustrates some of the process parameters that the team developed. This part of the doctor's office example also shows the relationship between the key technical requirements and the process parameters for those processes. The weight for the input row is determined by taking the final weight for the column from the planning matrix and dividing it by 10.

	Critical process specifications	Weight	System requirements	Scheduler requirements	Doctors' experience	Staffing system	Operator experience
System available		27	⊙			○	⊙
Care available		32		⊙	⊙	⊙	
Scheduler speed		9	⊙				△
Doctor training		22			⊙		
Doctor staff size		35				⊙	
Scheduler accuracy		40	△	⊙			○
Scheduler flexibility		33	○	⊙			
Doctor flexibility		40	○	○			△
System capability		40	⊙				
Operator training		37					⊙
System speed		13	⊙	△			△
Training process		33		○			⊙
Screening process		30		○			⊙
Insurance knowledge		17		○			⊙
Value			100 MHz	10 sec.	10 years	1 month	5 years
Direction			↑	↑	↑	○	↑
Weight			1020	1305	486	684	1416

Figure 12.6 The doctor's office process parameters.

EXERCISES

1. Using the information for the maid's process in making up rooms from chapter 11, develop the key process parameters and the key parts for the second room.

2. Determine how many different rooms you can develop for the doctor's office example and develop the input requirements for each of the rooms.

ENDNOTE

1. Ronald G. Day, *Quality Function Deployment: Linking a Company with Its Customers* (Milwaukee: ASQC Quality Press, 1993).

Part III

Strategic Applications

Chapter 13

Using Your Results for Strategic Decisions

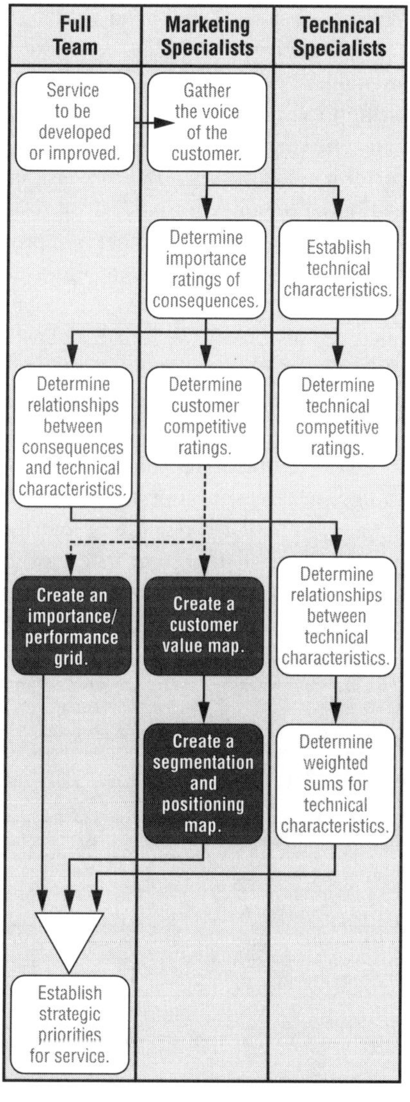

CHAPTER TOPICS

- Prioritizing Resource Allocations
- Value to the Customer
- Market Segmentation
- Brand Positioning

CHAPTER TOOLS

- Competitive Profile
- Importance–Performance Grid
- Customer Value Map
- Segmentation Map
- Positioning Map

We have looked at how to collect the voice of the customer and use it to develop outstanding services and operations in the prior chapters. Now we look at how to use this information to aid strategic decision making.

PRIORITIZING RESOURCE ALLOCATIONS

One very important strategic decision is where to allocate resources. Within our model, we need to decide what we should work on—which parts of the service process we should spend resources to improve. We use an importance–performance grid to help you prioritize your use of resources on improving the most critical customer benefits. While you can use the competitive profile we created in chapter 6 for this purpose, the importance–performance grid is straightforward, visual, and easily understood by everyone in the organization.

Let us look at the competitive profile[1] for pizza delivery that we developed in chapter 6, shown in Figure 13.1. Recall that once we have completed plotting the ratings for each brand on every consequence, we interpret the results. We look for gaps: gaps between our brand and the competition and gaps between our brand and the highest possible score, 5.0. If our brand is A, then we are behind the competition overall and have a higher price. This combination does not bode well for our future survival!

We see that we are ahead of the competition on "Crust is good" and "I can get my favorite toppings." On "Crust is good," we still have a considerable gap between our rating and the highest possible. Since this consequence is most important to consumers, we would want to improve our crust. This is a priority item for us. Our crust may be keeping us in business, but we do not want to depend on meeting this consequence alone.

Consequence	Mean Importance	Average Rating				
		1	2	3	4	5
Crust is good	9.7		B	C	A	
Order is taken quickly	6.6			A	C B	
Delivery is quick	8.1		A	BC		
I can get my favorite toppings	7.5			BC	A	
Pizza is hot when I get it	7.8			A	BC	
I can order when I want	6.5			AC	B	
I save money	8.3			A	B C	

Figure 13.1 Competitive profile for pizza delivery.

Brand A is behind the competition on "Order is taken quickly," "Delivery is quick," "I can order when I want," and "I save money." "Delivery is quick" and "I save money" are more important to customers than the other two, although not as important as "Crust is good." These would both be high priority items to work on providing. We should look at our delivery speed and at our pricing.

While we interpret the competitive profile for strategic allocation of resources, we have to consider several factors at once. The importance–performance grid[2] combines these factors for us. The grid has four quadrants based on two levels each of two dimensions: relative importance and relative performance. We draw the grid for one specific brand, in this chapter we again use brand A. We split the levels at the median value for each dimension.

Using the values in Table 6.1, repeated as Table 13.1, the median importance rating is 7.8, the middle importance rating when we place them in order. We plot the relative importance ratings on the vertical axis. We place consequences that we rated as more important than the median (crust is good, delivery is quick, save money, and pizza is hot) above the horizontal line representing the median importance rating. We place the other consequences below the median. (Note that "Pizza is hot" was rated exactly at the median, yet was placed above the line. We could justify a placement either above or below the line. Here, however, it is closely associated with "Delivery is quick," making placement in the same quadrant a rational choice.)

The mean brand rating on "Crust is good" is 3.4. Brand A scored above the median on this consequence, so we place "Crust is good" to the right of the vertical line representing the median brand rating. We calculate the median for each consequence to determine its position on the right or left of the vertical median line. Figure 13.2 shows the results.

Table 13.1 Brand ratings for pizza delivery.

Consequence	Mean Importance	Brand		
		A	B	C
The crust is good	9.7	4.1	2.9	3.4
Order is taken quickly	6.6	3.6	4.4	4.0
Delivery is quick	8.1	2.7	3.5	3.7
I can get my favorite toppings	7.5	4.2	3.5	3.5
Pizza is hot when I get it	7.8	3.8	4.0	4.1
I can order when I want	6.5	3.4	4.5	3.5
I save money	8.3	3.0	4.0	4.3

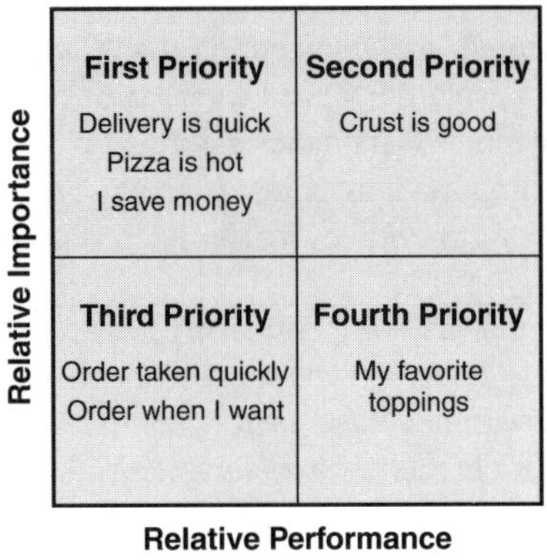

Figure 13.2 Importance–performance grid for brand A pizza delivery.

The same consequences stand out as priorities as in the competitive grid, but here the reader sees them easily without further analysis. Brand A needs to improve on "Delivery is quick," "Pizza is hot," and "I save money." It also needs to maintain or improve its performance on "Crust is good," where it performs relatively well. While the importance–performance grid does not show the gap between current brand performance and the top possible rating, it does indicate the relatively high priority of a good crust. This level of priority should lead us to look at our score on this consequence to see if we can improve on it.

"Order taken quickly" and "Order when I want" are lesser priorities for brand A. Allocating resources to improve on these will not provide as much benefit as working on the three consequences that were higher in importance. "I can get my favorite toppings" is the lowest priority for brand A. If we need to economize on anything, this would be the area in which to reduce costs. We are performing above average, but this consequence is not that important to consumers.

VALUE TO THE CUSTOMER

Both the competitive profile and the importance–performance grid indicated that brand A should work on saving customers money. Actual improvement on this consequence would require a price reduction; if cost reductions are not possible, then the profit margins will go down. Making this decision would be difficult and might be wrong. We have another strategic tool available to help us with this decision: the customer value map.[3]

A *customer value map* depicts the relationships between the brands' values as perceived by the customer. The two axes or dimensions of the customer value map are relative price and relative performance. We place each brand on the map in a position that shows its position relative to the other brands. To make these placements, we calculate ratios for each brand compared to the average of all brands.

First, we separate the price consequence(s) from the performance (non-price) consequences. Using the data from Table 6.2, we calculate a weighted sum of each brand's ratings on the performance and price consequences, as shown in Table 13.2. Next, we calculate the mean of the weighted sums across brands that are 170.4 for the performance consequences and 31.26 for price. Then we divide each weighted sum by the mean to get the ratios for the brands, as shown in Table 13.2.

Once we have these ratios calculated, we plot them on a graph with relative price on the vertical axis and relative performance on the horizontal, with the midpoints being the mean values. The price axis is plotted the opposite of normal so that a good price in the minds of the consumers is below the horizontal line. As a result, the brand that has the best combination of price and performance will be closest to the lower right corner. Figure 13.3 shows the results for pizza delivery.

Table 13.2 Weighted sums by brand for performance and price consequences.

	Brand:	A		B		C	
Consequence	**Importance**	**Rating**	**Weighted Rating**	**Rating**	**Weighted Rating**	**Rating**	**Weighted Rating**
The crust is good	9.7	4.1	39.77	2.9	28.13	3.4	32.98
Order is taken quickly	6.6	3.6	23.76	4.4	29.04	4.0	26.4
Delivery is quick	8.1	2.7	21.87	3.5	28.35	3.7	29.97
I can get my favorite toppings	7.5	4.2	31.50	3.5	26.25	3.5	26.25
Pizza is hot when I get it	7.8	3.8	29.64	4.0	31.20	4.1	31.98
I can order when I want	6.5	3.4	22.10	4.5	29.25	3.5	22.75
Sum			168.64		172.22		170.33
Ratio			**0.99**		**1.01**		**1.00**
I save money.	8.3	3.0	24.90	4.0	33.20	4.3	35.69
Ratio			**0.80**		**1.06**		**1.14**

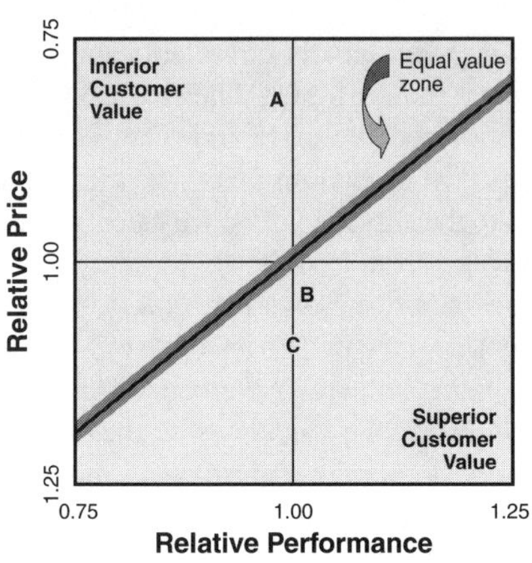

Figure 13.3 Customer value map for pizza delivery.

We added an equal value zone to the map. We determine its slope by the ratio of the importance of the performance consequences to the importance of the price consequences. For our pizza delivery example, the average importance of the performance consequences was 7.7, while the importance of price was 8.3. The ratio is 0.93, so the line slopes slightly more to the right than a line with slope 1.0. With this slope, a change in price will affect a brand's location relative to the equal value zone more than an equal change in performance. If brand A's rating on price increased by 0.20, it would fall in the equal value zone. If brand A's rating on performance increased by 0.20, it would still fall above the equal value zone in the inferior customer value zone.

Both brands B and C are perceived as better values by customers than brand A since they are closer to the lower right corner, with brand C representing the best value of the three. The managers of brand A can easily see that customers perceive it as an inferior value. According to the theory of Bradley T. Gale,[4] brand A will lose market share to brands B and C. He has supported his theory with several studies. In order to keep from losing market share, management must increase its perceived value in the eyes of its customers. They can decrease its price or increase its performance or a combination of both. From the slope of the equal value zone, they know that a change in price will have relatively more impact on perceived value. Now management has the information it needs to decide whether to decrease price.

MARKET SEGMENTATION

The above discussions about the competitive profile, the importance–performance grid, and the customer value map assumed that the data were collected from a homogeneous group of customers who all had the same needs and wants for pizza delivery and valued them the same (same importance ratings). We know that this is seldom the case. Once you have collected your importance ratings, the question is empirical: Does your data show significant variation in the importance ratings? If so, then you should segment your market, or in this case the group of customers you had, to rate importance of the consequences.

Happily, you have already collected the data you need to segment your customer group—the importance ratings on the consequences. For this step, you go back to your raw data, the actual individual importance ratings. If you have sophisticated statistical software with cluster analysis available,[5] then your computer can create the segments for you using the importance ratings for all consequences. If you do not have access to cluster analysis, you can create the segments from the raw data by hand.

Let us look at a portion of the raw data for the pizza delivery example in Table 13.3. The table shows the importance ratings for 14 respondents. The top importance rating for each respondent is in boldface and we grouped the respondents by the consequence that each indicated as most important.

The purpose in creating segments or groups is to have groups that are as much alike as possible within each group and as different as possible

Table 13.3 A portion of the importance ratings for pizza delivery.

Respondent	1	11	10	14	2	9	3	4	12	5	8	13	6	7
Crust is good	**10**	**10**	7	7	8	9	8	9	8	7	7	7	7	7
Order is taken quickly	6	6	6	6	7	5	6	5	6	6	6	5	5	5
Delivery is quick	8	7	**10**	**10**	**10**	7	7	8	9	9	8	6	7	7
I can get my favorite toppings	8	9	5	6	6	**10**	**10**	7	6	7	6	6	6	6
Pizza is hot when I get it	8	9	8	8	9	8	7	**10**	**10**	8	7	8	8	7
I can order when I want	6	4	5	7	6	5	6	5	6	**10**	**10**	**10**	5	8
I save money	6	5	7	6	6	6	5	6	5	5	6	8	**10**	**10**

between groups. Graphically, we want to separate the groups by as much distance as possible.

We could separate these 14 respondents into six groups as indicated by the consequence rated most important. However, looking at the data, we see that respondents who rated "Crust is good" high also rated "I can get my favorite toppings" high, and vice versa. Likewise, those who rated "Delivery is quick" high also rated "Pizza is hot when I get it" high, and vice versa. We can logically combine these two groups to yield four segments.

Although we have determined four segments, when we look at the segments graphically, we only use two dimensions. The choice of the two dimensions (consequences) to use makes a huge difference in what we discover. The best approach when creating a positioning map by hand is to try out all possible pairs of consequences to see which give the best segmentation. (Cluster analysis combines all consequences to give the best separation of groups.) A shortcut is to determine which two consequences show the greatest variation in scores, preferably based on the standard deviation.

Since we do not have all the data available to determine the standard deviation, we use the consequences with the greatest range of scores shown in Table 13.3. "I can order when I want" has the greatest range (4 to 10). Both "I save money" and "I can get my favorite toppings" have scores from 5 to 10. We will look at both of these in combination with "I can order when I want" to see which gives the best segments.

We represent each segment or group by a circle. We place the center of the circle at the point that represents the segment's average score on the two dimensions (consequences). The size of the circle represents the number of respondents or customers in the segment. Figures 13.4 and 13.5 show segmentation maps drawn from the data in Table 13.3.

In comparison, Figure 13.4 has the two largest segments very close together, while they are further apart in Figure 13.5. Therefore, we use Figure 13.5. Here we see that the largest segment rated the importance of both consequences in the middle range. The next largest segment rated toppings as very important, but rated order times in the middle range. The third largest segment rated order times as very important, but rated toppings in the middle range.

BRAND POSITIONING

Now that we have determined the locations of the market segments, we turn our attention to the position of the brands on the same consequences in the minds of the consumers. We use the data in Table 13.1 to position or place the brands on the map as customers perceive them. Again, we are

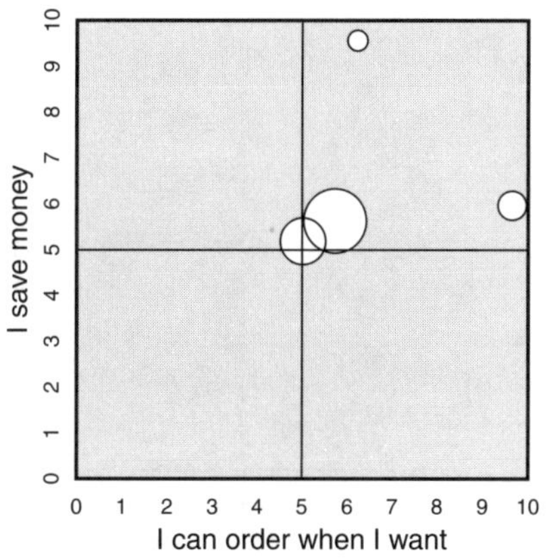

Figure 13.4 Segmentation map for pizza delivery.

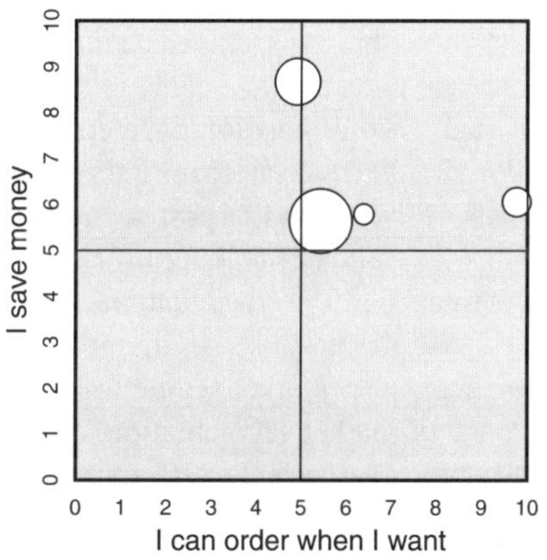

Figure 13.5 Alternative pizza delivery segmentation map.

simplifying, this time by assuming all the customers rated the brands about the same. We would really want to analyze how each of our market segments rated the brands to see if any significant differences exist.

We represent each brand by its name or a letter placed according to its average rating on the two dimensions (consequences). Since the brand rating scale of one to five differed from the importance rating scale of zero to 10, we have to adjust the scale to place the brands on the map. We think of each scale as going from one to five with the midline at three. Figure 13.6 shows the positioning map for our pizza delivery example.

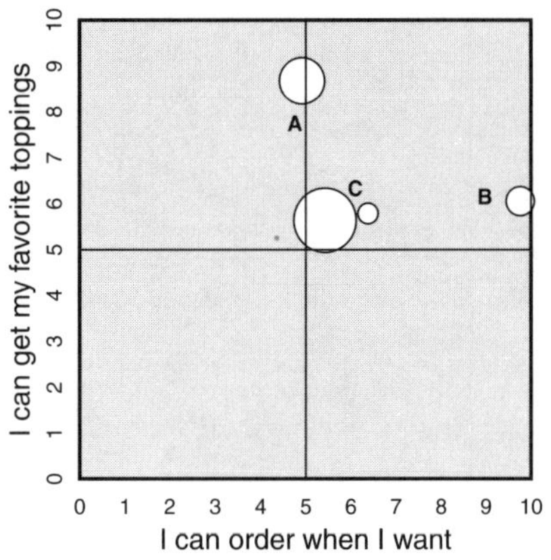

Figure 13.6 Positioning map for pizza delivery.

Interestingly, each of the brands seems to be meeting the needs of a different market segment, and each market segment has a brand that meets its needs fairly well. Based on this positioning map, we might change our minds on what brand A should do to improve. This map shows us that brand A could meet the needs of the second-largest segment better by increasing the number of toppings it offers and making no change in ordering times. The importance–performance grid told us that brand A should not improve on "favorite toppings." We based those results on the average of all customers, however, rather than on market segments. This contrast in results shows us the importance of market segmentation.

Management of brand A can select to target the second-largest market segment by increasing the number of toppings offered, or management can select to target the largest (and smallest) segment by decreasing its emphasis on toppings and working on some other consequences. If management selects the latter strategy, then brand A will go head to head with brand B for share of that market segment.

THE DOCTOR'S OFFICE

Figure 13.7 reproduces the competitive profile for the doctor's office originally shown in Figure 6.4. Taking a look at this profile strategically, the doctor's office needs to close the gap with its competition on "I am not put

Consequence	Mean Importance	Average Rating				
		1	2	3	4	5
I get an appointment within a week of my call	7.9		B		A	
I am not put on hold	7.3			A	B	
I am asked few needless questions	6.8		A	B		
I have my choice of days and times	9.6			B	A	
I spend little time on the phone	8.2			A	B	
Overall, I am satisfied with the appointment process				B A		

Figure 13.7 Competitive profile for the doctor's office.

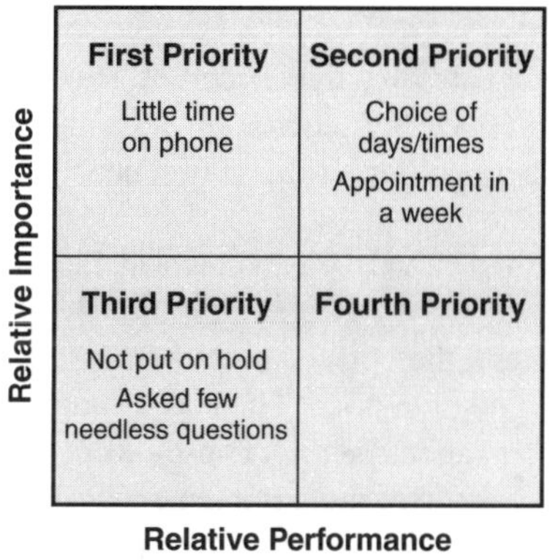

Figure 13.8 Importance–performance grid for the doctor's office.

on hold," "I am asked few needless questions," and "I spend little time on the phone." Of these, the last one had the highest importance rating, so improvement in it is most critical to the office. The office staff needs to look into the causes of keeping people on the phone when they call in for appointments to see if they can reduce that time requirement.

The office staff used the brand ratings for the doctor's office shown in Figure 6.3 to create the importance–performance grid shown in Figure 13.8. This grid shows the same consequence as being most important, "I spend little time on the phone." Again, the office staff needs to improve in this

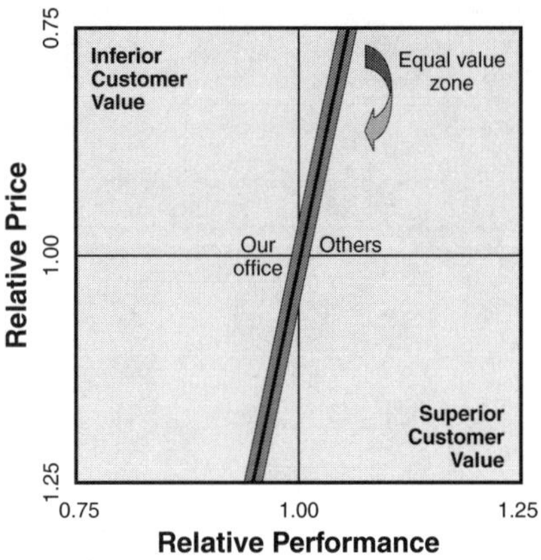

Figure 13.9 Customer value map for doctor's office.

area. The grid also indicates that the office staff should maintain or improve its performance on "I have my choice of days and times" and "I get an appointment within a week of my call," consequences that are in the second-priority quadrant.

Using the weighted brand sums shown in Figure 6.3, the staff completed the customer value map shown in Figure 13.9. Since pricing at medical offices is consistent, they placed both their office and the other offices at the median line on relative price. The equal value zone was set at a very steep angle since most patients are not conscious of the prices of office visits, due to medical coverage of most standard costs. The doctor's office and the other offices were very close in relative performance, with the others scoring a small amount higher. With the steepness of the equal value zone, this would place the other offices in the superior customer value zone. The results of this analysis are not highly significant.

The staff of the doctor's office was not interested in segmenting the patient marketplace, so they did not complete a segmentation/positioning map.

EXERCISE

Using the data you collected for the exercises in chapters 5 and 6, create an importance–performance grid, a customer value map, and a segmentation-position map.

ENDNOTES

1. Robert B. Woodruff and Sarah F. Gardial, *Know Your Customer: New Approaches to Understanding Customer Value and Satisfaction* (Cambridge, MA: Blackwell, 1996).
2. John A. Martilla and John C. James, "Importance–Performance Analysis," *Journal of Marketing* 41, no. 1 (1977): 77–79.
3. Bradley T. Gale, *Managing Customer Value: Creating Quality and Service that Customers Can See* (New York: The Free Press, 1994).
4. Ibid.
5. Statistical Package for the Social Sciences (SPSS) or SAS, for examples.

Chapter 14

An Example: A Laundry and Dry Cleaning Service

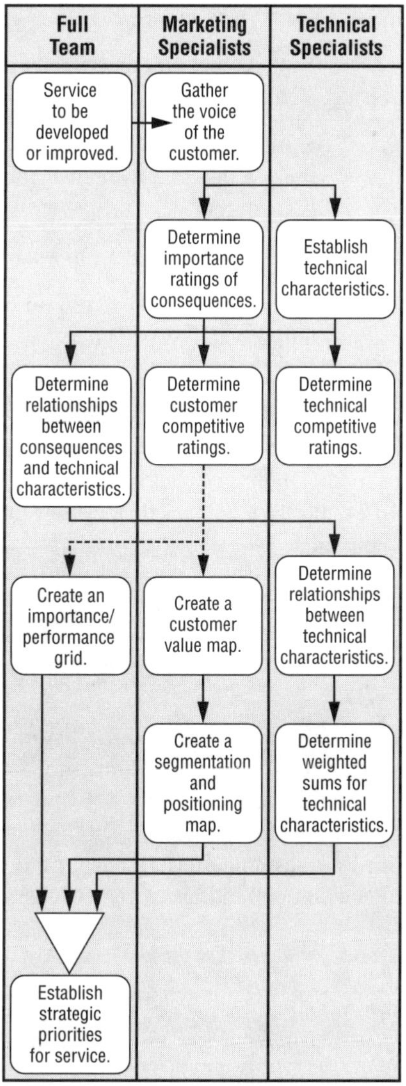

CHAPTER TOPICS

- Voice of the Customer
- Importance and Competitive Analysis
- Technical Requirements
- Developing Service Processes
- Selecting Marketing Priorities and Strategies

CHAPTER TOOLS

- Customer Interviews
- Attribute/Consequence Grid
- Importance Questionnaire
- Customer Competitive Assessment
- Competitive Grid
- Technical Requirements
- Relationship Matrix
- Competitive Technical Assessment
- Priority Technical Requirements
- House of Quality
- Importance–Performance Grid
- Customer Value Map
- Segmentation and Positioning Map

In this chapter, we present an example using all the techniques described in this book. The example, for a laundry and dry cleaning service, comes from a project completed by students of the authors as a class project.*

VOICE OF THE CUSTOMER

The first step was to interview customers of the laundry and dry cleaning service to obtain their voice. The students used four basic questions during the interviews:

1. What comes to mind when you think of laundry and dry cleaning services?
2. How would you describe the type of laundry and dry cleaning service that you use now? Why do you choose service from that company?
3. What do you want from a laundry and dry cleaning service?
4. What happens when you do not get good service from your laundry and dry cleaners?

They followed up each of these questions with multiple probes, asking why each answer was important to the customer. They extracted the consequences from transcripts of these interviews. After grouping the data from the interviews and eliminating duplicates, they ended up with 30 different consequences that they grouped into four categories, as shown in Table 14.1.

IMPORTANCE AND COMPETITIVE ANALYSIS

Once they had completed the list of consequences (and some attributes), they selected one major competitor for the laundry and dry cleaners. (They tried for a third, but could not find enough people who were aware of the third company's services to complete the questionnaire.) Then they developed a questionnaire to measure the importance of the consequences and the customers' ratings of the two establishments. They administered these

* The authors wish to acknowledge and thank Mary Ann Beam, William E. Railey, and Robert D. Brient for allowing us to use their class project as an example in this book.

Table 14.1 Consequences for a laundry and dry cleaners.

Group	Consequence
Quality	My clothes are not burned or stained
	My clothes are not wrinkled
	My clothes have no remaining dirt or stains
	My clothes have no shrinkage
	My clothes have no chemical smell
	My clothes have no broken buttons
	My laundry is completely done
	My clothes are neatly folded or hung
	My clothes have no loose or missing buttons
	My clothes have the correct amount of starch
	My pants are not placed on skinny hangers
	The laundry cleans delicate fabrics and rugs
Service	None of my laundry is missing
	My laundry is ready when promised
	The laundry offers standard overnight service
	I do not wait longer than 3–5 minutes for service
	I wait in line behind no more than two customers
	The laundry offers one-hour speedy service
	The laundry offers pick-up and delivery
	The clerks do not blame me for poor cleaning quality
	The clerks are courteous
	The laundry offers value-added services, like sewing on buttons, hems, etc.
	The clerks are neat and clean
Location	The laundry has easy access for parking
	The laundry is located on a major road near other shopping
	The laundry has a drive-through for drop-off and pickup
Price	The price is no more than $1 per hanger
	The price is no more than $12 for 8 lbs of laundry
	The laundry offers discount cards for repeat customers
	The laundry offers discount coupons

questionnaires to a number of customers of the laundry services, then tabulated the responses and calculated averages. Table 14.2 shows the results.

From the data in Table 14.2, they created a competitive grid, shown in Figure 14.1. They put the consequences in order of importance to make interpretation of the results easier. Looking down the rows, they could see that the first area that was a great concern was the perception that clothes

Table 14.2 Questionnaire results.

#	Consequence	Importance Rating	Brand Rating A	Brand Rating B
1	My clothes are not burned or stained	8.70	4.5	3.5
2	None of my laundry is missing	8.65	4.0	4.0
3	My clothes are not wrinkled	8.35	4.3	3.5
4	My clothes have no remaining dirt or stains	7.87	3.6	3.5
5	My clothes have no shrinkage	7.61	4.0	2.5
6	My clothes have no chemical smell	7.43	4.3	2.5
7	My clothes have no broken buttons	7.26	3.5	3.5
8	The laundry has easy access for parking	7.13	4.4	4.0
9	The clerks are courteous	7.04	4.1	3.5
10	My laundry is completely done	7.00	4.1	4.0
11	My clothes are neatly folded or hung	6.87	3.8	4.0
12	My clothes have no loose or missing buttons	6.78	3.8	2.5
13	The clerks do not blame me for poor cleaning quality	6.61	4.0	3.0
14	My laundry is ready when promised	6.48	4.4	4.0
15	The laundry offers standard overnight service	6.17	3.8	4.0
16	The laundry is located on a major road near other shopping	6.13	3.8	3.0
17	The clerks are neat and clean	5.96	4.4	3.5
18	The laundry offers value-added services, like sewing on buttons, hems, etc.	5.78	3.9	4.0
19	The price is no more than $1 per hanger	5.74	2.1	1.5
20	I do not wait longer than 3–5 minutes for service	5.61	4.0	4.0
21	My clothes have the correct amount of starch	5.57	3.9	3.0
22	The laundry has a drive-through for drop-off and pickup	5.52	4.1	1.5
23	I wait in line behind no more than two customers	5.22	4.0	4.0
24	My pants are not placed on skinny hangers	5.04	3.9	1.5
25	The laundry cleans delicate fabrics and rugs	4.78	3.8	3.5
26	The price is no more than $12 for 8 lbs. of laundry	4.65	2.9	3.0
27	The laundry offers one-hour speedy service	4.39	3.4	4.0
28	The laundry offers discount cards for repeat customers	4.26	2.0	2.5
29	The laundry offers pickup and delivery	4.09	2.1	1.5
30	The laundry offers discount coupons	3.91	2.6	2.5
		6.02	3.6	3.06

	Consequence	Imp.	1	2	3	4	5
1	My clothes are not burned or stained	8.70			B	A	
2	None of my laundry is missing	8.65				AB	
3	My clothes are not wrinkled	8.35			B	A	
4	My clothes have no remaining dirt or stains	7.87			BA		
5	My clothes have no shrinkage	7.61		B		A	
6	My clothes have no chemical smell	7.43		B		A	
7	My clothes have no broken buttons	7.26			AB		
8	The laundry has easy access for parking	7.13				B A	
9	The clerks are courteous	7.04		B	A		
10	My laundry is completely done	7.00				BA	
11	My clothes are neatly folded or hung	6.87			A	B	
12	My clothes have no loose or missing buttons	6.78		B	A		
13	The clerks do not blame me for poor cleaning quality	6.61			B	A	
14	My laundry is ready when promised	6.48				B A	
15	The laundry offers standard overnight service	6.17			A	B	
16	The laundry is located on a major road near other shopping	6.13			B A		
17	The clerks are neat and clean	5.96		B	A		
18	The laundry offers value-added services, like sewing on buttons, hems, etc.	5.78		B	A		
19	The price is no more than $1 per hanger	5.74	B	A			
20	I do not wait longer than 3–5 minutes for service	5.61				AB	
21	My clothes have the correct amount of starch	5.57			B A		
22	The laundry has a drive-through for drop-off and pickup	5.52	B		A		
23	I wait in line behind no more than two customers	5.22				AB	
24	My pants are not placed on skinny hangers	5.04	B		A		
25	The laundry cleans delicate fabrics and rugs	4.78			B A		
26	The price is no more than $12 for 8 lbs. of laundry	4.65		A	B		
27	The laundry offers one-hour speedy service	4.39			A	B	
28	The laundry offers discount cards for repeat customers	4.26		A B			
29	The laundry offers pickup and delivery	4.09	B	A			
30	The laundry offers discount coupons	3.91		BA			

Figure 14.1 Competitive grid.

had remaining dirt or stains, where the cleaners scored less than four. Broken buttons was another area of great concern because of the cleaner's rating and its importance. The next critical areas were courteousness of the clerks, clothes being neatly folded or hung, and loose or missing buttons.

To complete the customer portion of the house, they could look at the customer complaints received in the past six months, if the organization kept track of them, and categorize them according to the consequences listed. Then they determined the number of complaints related to each consequence. We generally insert this complaint information into the house just to the left of the customer competitive ratings. That completed the customer portion of the house of quality.

TECHNICAL REQUIREMENTS

Once the customer portion of the house of quality was completed, they began the technical portion. The first step was to brainstorm technical requirements that could result in delivering each consequence. They used tree and cause-and-effect diagrams to help them determine the technical requirements. Table 14.3 shows the technical requirements they determined along with the direction of improvement and the unit of measurement.

After determining the technical requirements, the students turned their attention to the critical relationships between the consequences and the technical requirements. They identified three levels of relationship: strong ⊙, medium ○, and weak △. This part of the house of quality took careful consideration. The team worked as a group to decide on the critical relationships. Figure 14.2 shows part of the matrix of relationships using the key given in this paragraph.

Next, the team of students turned its attention to the technical competitive ratings and operational targets. If the team members are very familiar with all the competitors to be rated, then the team may be able to rate the competitors in a meeting using group consensus. A more objective method for obtaining technical competitive ratings is to use mystery shoppers who take similar laundry/dry cleaning orders, such as three shirts and a pair of trousers, to each of the competitors. The mystery shoppers rate each establishment on all the technical requirements on a standardized form. On this project, the team used consensus and arrived at the technical ratings and operational targets partially shown in Figure 14.3.

After completing the technical competitive assessment, the team looked at the relationships between the technical requirements to determine both positive and negative correlations. Of particular concern were the negative

Table 14.3 Technical requirements.

Technical Requirement	Better Is:	Measurement
Pressing pressure	Target	Pounds
Pressing temperature	Target	Degrees
Pressing time	Target	Minutes
Solid contents in solvent	Target	Parts per liter
Solid contents in rinse	Target	Parts per liter
Cleaning temperature	Target	Degrees
Cleaning process time	Target	Minutes
Starch content	Target	Percent
Standard laundry cycle time	↓	Minutes
Standard dry cleaning cycle time	↓	Minutes
Quick service laundry cycle time	↓	Minutes
Quick service dry cleaning cycle time	↓	Minutes
Number of desk employees on duty	Target	Number
Number of trained desk employees	Target	Number
% laundry employees trained to handle desk	↑	Percent
Number of laundry employees	Target	Number
Uniforms required	Yes	Yes/No
Uniforms provided	Yes	Yes/No
Number of uniforms per week	↑	Number
Average time to take customer order	↓	Minutes
Average time to return customer order	↓	Minutes
Average waiting time	↓	Minutes
Offer pickup and delivery	Yes/No	Yes/No
Offer delicate cleaning	Yes/No	Yes/No
Offer rug cleaning	Yes/No	Yes/No
Offer one-hour service	Yes/No	Yes/No
Offer seamstress services	Yes/No	Yes/No
Laundry tracking system	Yes/No	Yes/No
Hanger types available	↑	Number
Average employee training hours	Target	Hours
% employees with customer service training	↑	Percent
Parking spots available	↑	Number
Located on major road	Yes/No	Yes/No
Located near shopping area	Yes/No	Yes/No
Drive-thru lane provided	Yes/No	Yes/No
Offer repeat customer cards	Yes/No	Yes/No
Offer discounts	Yes/No	Yes/No

Consequence	Imp.	Pressing pressure	Pressing temperature	Pressing time	Solid contents in solvent	Solid contents in rinse	Cleaning temperature	Cleaning process time	Starch conttent	Standard laundry cycle time	Standard dry cleaning cycle time	Quick service laundry cycle time	Quick service dry cleaning cycle time	Number or desk employees on duty	Number or trained desk employees	% laundry employees trained to handle desk	Number of laundry employees	Uniforms required	Number of uniforms per week
		⊙	⊙	⊙	⊙	⊙	⊙	⊙	⊙	↓	↓	↓	↓	⊙	⊙	↑	⊙	⊙	↑
No burns or stains on clothes	8.7	△	○	⊙	○	○	△	△											
No wrinkles	8.4	⊙	⊙	⊙					○										
No remaining dirt or stains	7.9				○	○	⊙	⊙											
No garment shrinkage	7.6		○	○	△		⊙	○											
No smell—especially chemical	7.4				⊙	⊙	△	⊙	△										
No broken buttons	7.3	⊙	△	△															
No partly done laundry	7.0			○	○	○	⊙	⊙	△	⊙	⊙	⊙	⊙						
Clothes folded or hung neatly	6.9			○															
No loose or missing buttons	6.8	⊙	○	○															
Not too much or too little starch	5.6	△	△	△					⊙										
No missing laundry	8.7																		
No late laundry	6.5																		
Standard service is overnight	6.2									⊙	⊙						⊙		
No service wait longer than 3–5 minutes	5.6													⊙	⊙	⊙			
No more than two customers in line	5.2																		
Speedy one-hour service	4.4											⊙	⊙				⊙		
Pickup and delivery	4.1																		
No blaming customers for poor quality	6.6													○	○	○			
Clerks are courteous	7.0													⊙	⊙	⊙			
Value-added services	5.8																		
Clerks are neat and clean	6.0																	⊙	⊙

Figure 14.2 Relationship matrix.

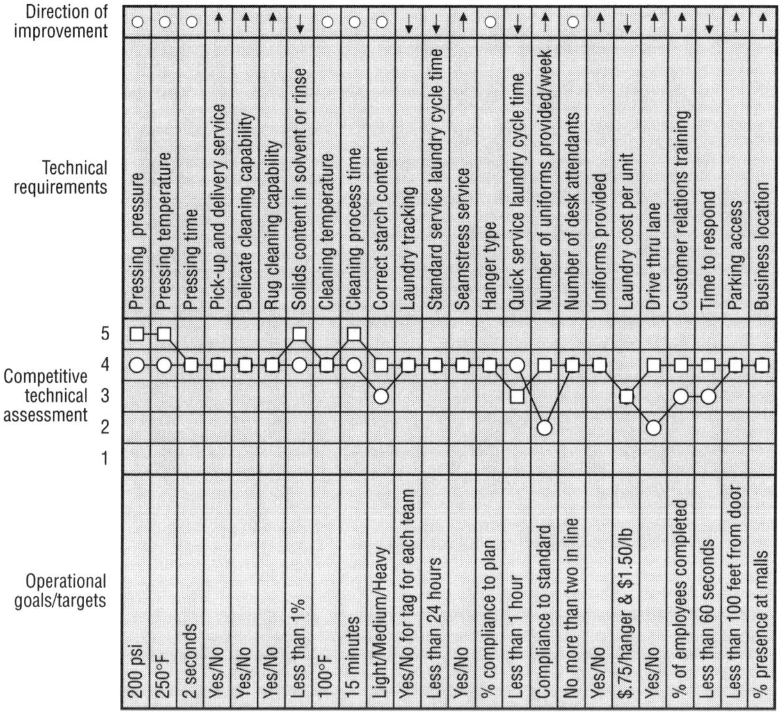

Figure 14.3 Competitive technical assessment.

correlations that indicate a needed trade-off between requirements; if one improves, the other gets worse. Figure 14.4 shows the technical requirement correlations.

DEVELOPING SERVICE PROCESSES

After completing the customer and technical portions of the house of quality, the team looked at what items should receive priority attention in developing or improving service processes. They used a spreadsheet to multiply the level of relationship between a technical requirement and each customer consequence (requirement) times the importance rating for that consequence, then summed these multiples to determine a total column weight for the technical requirement. They then rank-ordered the technical requirements to decide which they should carry forward to process development. They found the priorities listed in Table 14.4.

Figure 14.5 shows most of the final house of quality.

Table 14.4 Priority technical requirements.

Priority	Requirement	Total Column Weight
1	Pressing time	309
2	Cleaning process time	309
3	Cleaning temperature	253
4	Pressing temperature	241
5	Solids content in solvent	207
6	Pressing pressure	201
7	Quick service laundry cycle time	198
8	Standard laundry cycle time	171
9	Laundry tracking system	144
10	Customer relations training	144

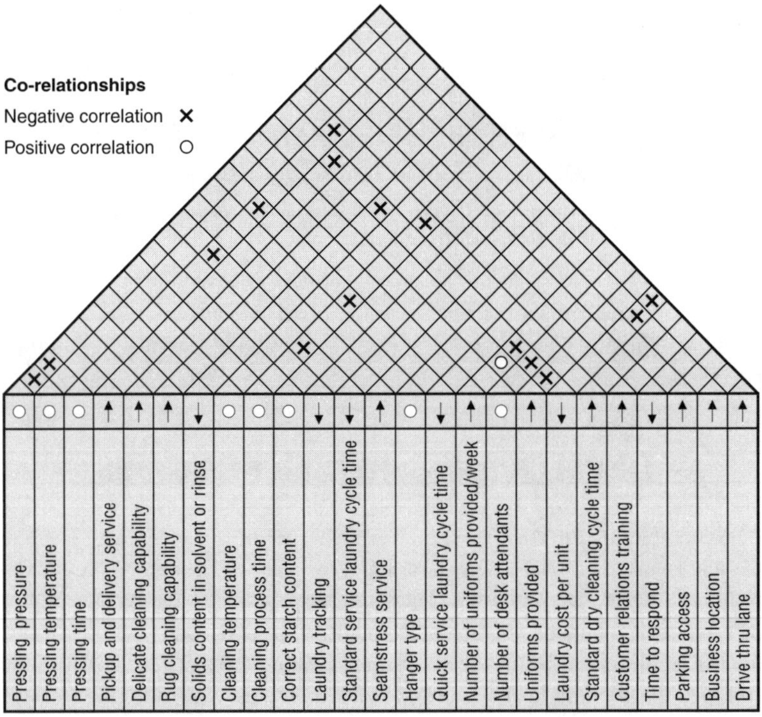

Figure 14.4 Requirement correlations.

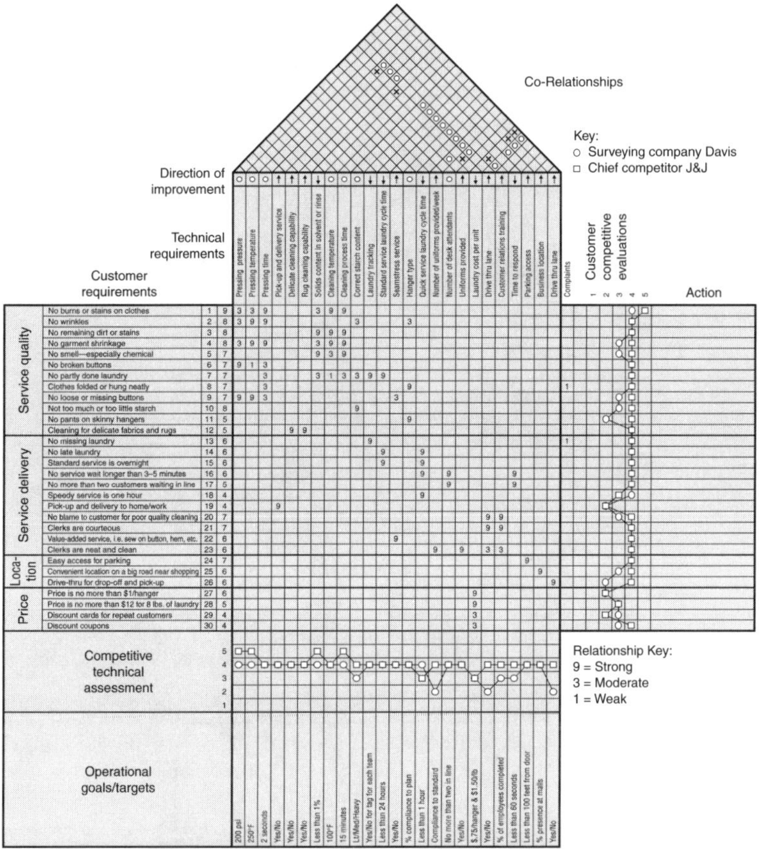

Figure 14.5 Completed house of quality.

SELECTING MARKETING PRIORITIES AND STRATEGIES

The other approach to looking at priorities used by the team was the importance–performance grid, shown in Figure 14.6. For each consequence, they determined whether it was above average in importance, and they determined whether firm A performed better or worse than firm B based on the data in Table 14.2. Using these calculations, they placed each consequence in a quadrant of the importance–performance grid.

The first-priority consequences are those that are important to consumers and on which consumers rated firm A as lower on delivery. Firm A

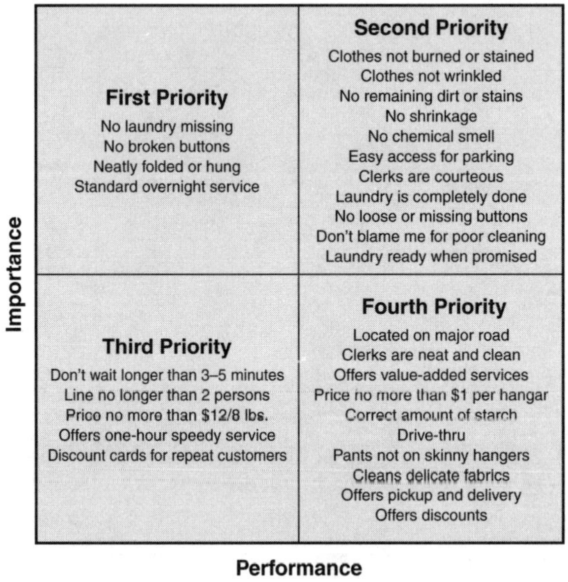

Figure 14.6 The importance–performance grid.

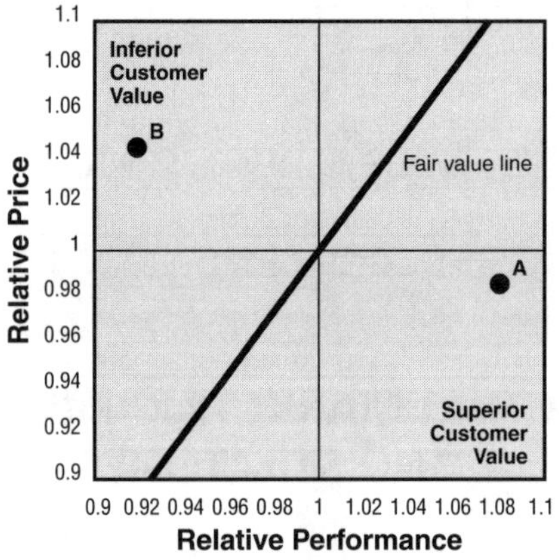

Figure 14.7 Customer value map.

needs to work on improving these items more than any others. Taking these items and going back to the relationship matrix in Figure 14.2, they looked at the technical requirements that were highly correlated with these consequences. (Note that some technical requirements are missing from Figure 14.2 due to space limitations.) They discovered that pressing pressure, standard laundry and dry cleaning cycle time, number of laundry employees, number of training hours per laundry employee, the laundry tracking system, and the variety of hanger types available were most critical. These differ from what they found using the total column weights shown in Table 14.4, primarily because the customer competitive ratings are included in this analysis and not in the total column weights. In addition, the importance–performance grid also does not include the effects of the relationships with other consequences. Both are worthy analyses to conduct and we should consider both their results when selecting priority requirements.

Chapter 15

Making the Business Case

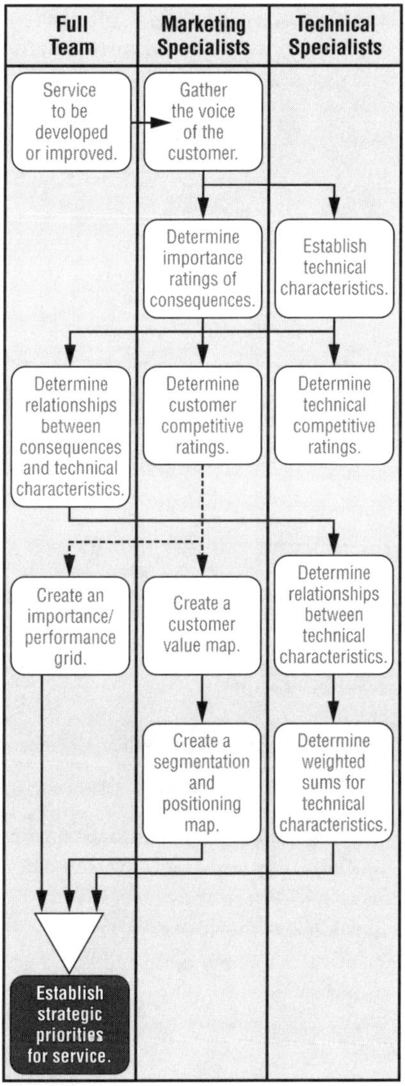

CHAPTER TOPICS

- Cost Savings
- Cycle-Time Reduction
- Customer Satisfaction, Retention, and Loyalty
- Lifetime Value of a Customer
- Increased Sales
- Greater Profits
- Strategic Competitive Advantage

CHAPTER TOOLS

- Cost of Quality
- Cost–Benefit Analysis
- Return on Investment
- Lifetime Value of a Customer

Quality function deployment (QFD) has proven to be a powerful process that brings significant results to organizations of all types. The results from other organizations rarely sell a business on using the process itself until it sees the results it can have. Demonstrating the results of using QFD is critical to its acceptance and continued use within an organization. The results that can be demonstrated include: lower development costs; shorter development cycle times; greater customer satisfaction, retention, and loyalty; increased sales; greater profits; and a strategic competitive advantage. To make the case for continued use of QFD in your organization, you need to collect the data and demonstrate as many of these results as possible for your first—and every—QFD project. Let us look at how to gather data for some of these outcomes.

COST SAVINGS

Cost savings can come from the design process itself or from implementing the new service. To demonstrate either of these, you need data from the "before" situation, either from prior service design processes or from the old service.

If your organization has records of previous design processes, or you can reconstruct these processes, then you want to determine the following:

- Number of hours required for total design process and cost
- Amount of rework of design steps and cost
- Number of revisions to design and costs
- Number of scrapped prototypes and costs
- Number of complaints about service and costs
  - Refunds
  - Projected lost repeat sales
- Number of nonconformances to regulations or standards and costs

Collect this cost information from as many prior service designs as you can. You may need to estimate costs using hourly salaries plus benefits of those involved in the process. We cover estimating the cost of loss of repeat sales later in this chapter.

You may have collected some of this data as part of a cost of quality[1,2] analysis. Cost of quality is the total costs required to provide a high-quality product to your customer. It includes rework, scrap, returns, and other costs associated with eliminating defective services.

Once you have this data, you can average it for the prior design process, and then compare the average to the costs of your service design using the QFD approach. The difference represents your organization's cost savings.

CYCLE-TIME REDUCTION

Along with collecting information on dollar costs, collect information on cycle time: the number of days taken from the start of a service design project until it is completed and implemented. Again, determine cycle time for as many prior service designs as possible, using data from prior records or reconstructing cycle time from the collective memory of organization members. Determine an average and compare your cycle time using QFD to that average to determine your savings.

Manufacturing companies have found that the QFD approach reduces design cycle time significantly.[3] For example, automobile manufacturers have reduced design times for a new automobile from seven to three years.

CUSTOMER SATISFACTION, RETENTION, AND LOYALTY

We can best measure customer satisfaction with a questionnaire. If you have a standard satisfaction questionnaire with a data history, then you can use that as your baseline. After you have implemented your new service, use the existing questionnaire to measure satisfaction and compare the new ratings with the historical baseline.

If you do not have an existing questionnaire or would like to improve your questionnaire, then you can develop it based on the information you collected in chapters 5 through 7. You want to write questions for the consequences that your customers and potential customers rated as important. A good guide is to have questions for each high-priority area on the importance–performance grid you developed in chapter 13. You eliminate questions on areas that were not of high priority according to the same grid, unless they relate to another area of current strategic importance to your organization.

Customer retention can be more difficult to measure. If you have a small number of customers, you may find the data you need in your existing records. What you want to do is enumerate the customers you had during a specific time period, such as the prior quarter. The time period you select for comparison should be the length of the normal buying cycle for your service. If customers normally buy once a year, then the time period would be one year.

After you have enumerated your customers for that time period, then you determine which of those customers purchased again in the following period. Calculate the percentage of customers who bought again—that is your retention rate. You need to determine retention rates before and after the change in your service to see what improvement you have made.

Measuring loyalty is more complex than measuring either satisfaction or retention, partially because loyalty encompasses so many behaviors. Customer loyalty defines behavior in five areas: loyalty to the company, lack of propensity to switch, willingness to pay more, lack of external responses to problems, and internal responses to problems. Each of these has sub-areas that can be measured as indicators of loyalty.[4, 5]

First, loyalty to the company can include saying positive things about a company to other people, recommending the company to someone who seeks advice, encouraging friends and relatives to do business with the company, considering the company as first choice, and intending to do more business with the company in the next few years. Propensity to switch means doing less business with the company in the next few years and taking some of your business to a competitor that offers prices that are more attractive. Willingness to pay more includes continuing to do business with the company even if its price increases somewhat, or paying a higher price than competitors charge for the benefits you currently receive from the company. External responses to problems may be switching to a competitor, complaining to other consumers, or complaining to external agencies, such as the Better Business Bureau, if you experience a problem with the company's services. In contrast, internal responses to problems means complaining to the company's employees if a problem is experienced with the company's services.

Direct measurement of all aspects of loyalty is difficult, so they are usually measured as items on a questionnaire that ask about a customer's behavioral intentions in these areas. The most commonly used are:

- I plan to purchase from this company again in the future.
- I will recommend this company to my friends and family.

Customer relationship management (CRM), a current hot area in business circles, is an attempt to increase customer loyalty. It is all about increasing the value delivered to each customer, nurturing the relationship, to assure that the customer becomes and remains loyal. One reason that customer loyalty and customer relationship management are so important is that they increase the lifetime value of a customer.

LIFETIME VALUE OF A CUSTOMER

The lifetime value of a customer is an important concept when trying to determine the outcomes of any change in a service. The lifetime value of a customer is the expected profits from a customer over the time that customer continues to buy from the company.[6] To determine lifetime value, you need to know the average purchase cycle of the customer (or the average number of purchases per year), the average expected remaining lifetime of the customer, and the average profits per purchase. Then, multiply the average number of purchases per year times the average profits per purchase times the average remaining lifetime of a customer. The result is the lifetime value of purchases from a customer.

You can multiply this value by one plus the average number of friends and relatives that one loyal customer will refer to include the impact of word-of-mouth referrals (one of the other indicators of loyalty). Table 15.1 shows an example.

If you can estimate the number of customers who are being lost each year, then you can estimate the potential savings from improving the process. The number lost is the opposite of retention, described earlier in this chapter. The number of customers who purchased from you one year but not during the second is the number lost.

Table 15.1 Calculation of potential savings from customer retention.

Purchases oil changes per year	2
Profit margin per oil change	$2.00
Profit margin per year	$4.00
Remaining years as a customer	25
Profit margin from customer purchases	$100
Referrals per customer plus one	3
Profit margin per loyal customer	$300
Number of customers lost per year	300
Potential savings	**$90,000**

INCREASED SALES

The potential savings from retaining customers comes from a reduction in lost customers. Increased sales come from increasing loyalty through greater value delivery and satisfaction of customers. Existing customers may buy from you more often. Perhaps they are splitting their purchases between competitors; you may be able to capture a greater percentage of their purchases. Another possibility is to get your existing customers to buy other services from you, perhaps tune-ups for the garage for which Table 15.1 shows the data. Alternatively, customers who are not recommending you to others at present may begin doing so. You would estimate the value of these increased sales similarly to how we calculated potential savings in Table 15.1.

GREATER PROFITS

Greater profits come not only from decreased costs, potential savings, and increased sales, but also from the ability to raise prices. If you improve your services in ways that increase their perceived value to customers, then you can raise your prices (and profits) and still maintain or gain market share. The customer value map you learned about in chapter 13 illustrates how the price/performance trade-off works. You want to maintain or increase your distance below the equal value zone. The more you increase the perceived value of your service, the more you can increase your price and still maintain or improve your position.

To calculate the potential greater profits from improving your services, estimate the amount you can increase your price. Sometimes people try to add an item to a questionnaire asking customers how much more they would be willing to pay; however, the responses to these items are not very reliable measures of actual responses to price increases. The customer value map is the basis for an estimate of how much you can raise your price. Multiply your sales per year by the amount you estimate you can raise your price (assuming no additional costs) to estimate additional profits from improved services. Add this to the additional profits from decreased costs, potential savings from greater retention, and increased sales to calculate the total potential increased profits.

STRATEGIC COMPETITIVE ADVANTAGE

Strategic competitive advantage is the most difficult outcome to express in dollars. Your strategic competitive advantage comes from your new customer knowledge base. This base allows you to lead the competition with improved services, rather than following others, because you can anticipate future customer needs. Looking at the consequences and values that are important to customers, you can use the QFD approach to creatively develop new ways to increase the perceived value of your services. Once you have gone through one set of service changes, you can go back to your QFD house and determine the next most important areas to change. Although you should update the customer voice regularly, the knowledge you gained about your customers is robust and provides you with potential improvements for several years.

ENDNOTES

1. David S. Ang and Charles E. Hegji, "Quality Costs and Profits," *Southern Business Review* 23, no. 2 (1997): 1–10.
2. Lakshmi Tatikonda and Rao J. Tatikonda, "Measuring and Reporting the Cost of Quality," *Production and Inventory Management Journal* 37, no. 2 (1996): 1–8.
3. Ronald G. Day, *Quality Function Deployment: Linking a Company with Its Customers* (Milwaukee: ASQC Quality Press, 1993).
4. A. Parasuraman, Valarie A. Zeithaml, and Leonard L. Berry, "SERVQUAL: A Multiple-Item Scale for Measuring Consumer Perceptions of Service Quality," *Journal of Retailing* 64, no. 1 (1988): 12–40.
5. A. Parasuraman, Valarie A. Zeithaml, and Leonard L. Berry, "Moving Forward in Service Quality Research: Measuring Different Customer-Expectation Levels, Comparing Alternative Scales, and Examining the Performance–Behavioral Intentions Link," *Marketing Science Institute*, working paper report number 94-114, 1994.
6. Gary W. Henderson, "Ben & Jerry's Recipe," *Customer Service Management* (Nov/Dec 1999).

Chapter 16

Conclusions

CHAPTER TOPICS

- Concluding Comments on the Process
- The Process Tools Used
- The Process Flow from VOC to QFD

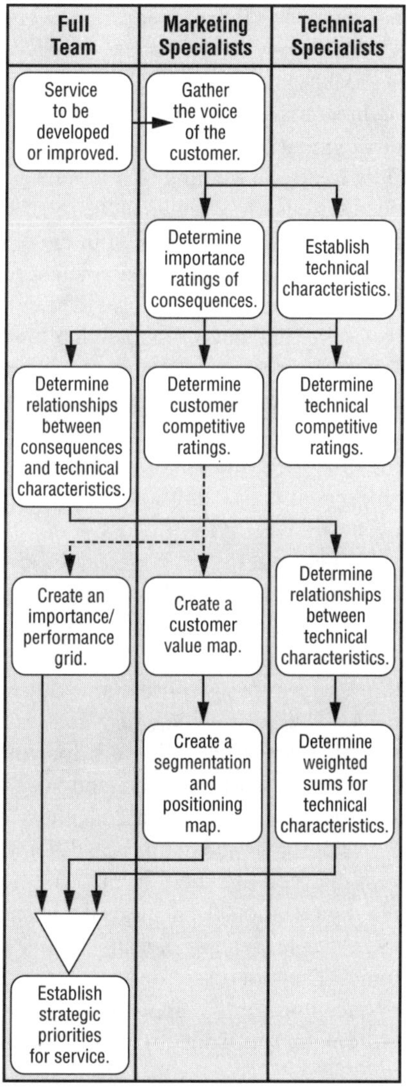

The power of linking the customers' voice to the internal organization should have become apparent with completion of the chapters of our book. You can derive methods to achieve customer satisfaction by focusing on obtaining customer needs from the direct users of the service. The start of our process is to define the customers and market and then determine the best methods to obtain their input verbatim—the voice of the customer. The tools used in this process have been around for many years and organizations have used them in many applications. We have shown how to use the tools to provide the right customer information to the internal personnel of the organization who are working on process development. This will provide the services needed by the various customers.

Many manufacturing organizations that provide services to customers in direct and indirect ties with their products have used the quality function deployment (QFD) process. Organizations have also applied QFD successfully to design training of internal services, using the various departments' needs as customer inputs to the process. In many applications, suppliers and even customers participated in the development of the QFD house to help develop the key process parameters required to meet the customers' needs. In many cases, suppliers provided input to the design process regarding the feasibility and costs of supplying inputs to the service.

Many companies find that the functions or features of the process they are developing have key characteristics that they must maintain or control to assure that they provide consistent service to their customers. For existing processes, the use of the QFD house helps to determine which parameters the company did not design properly and what they must redefine in the customer service process.

The input to this book came from years of experience with the application of our approach in the service industries and in the teaching of a masters program at Loyola University New Orleans. The specific approach you take to understand customers' needs and expectations will depend on the services that you provide and the customer base that you are trying to reach. The answers can vary and we have covered every specific application. The approach will work for you if you consider the differences that exist in your customer base and your service. Apply these concepts to your service design using your customers' input.

The tools used in this book should be familiar to the reader and we suggest that you use them in the establishment of your customers' input into the organization. To achieve the customer satisfaction that you must attain to be the leader in your chosen market, you must first focus on the customer. The tools used for the voice of the customer include the development of questions for the input needs. This area requires that you first address the customers you want to serve (market segmentation) and then develop a strategy for the information that you want to obtain from the interview, survey, or focus group. Someone who understands research methods, including interviews, focus groups, and survey design, is best at developing the questions. You may want to obtain outside professional help in this area. Brainstorming, affinity diagrams, relationship diagrams, interviewing techniques, focus group planning, and data sampling plans are all needed to be successful at discerning true customer needs and expectations. The various ways of prioritizing the customers wants (discussed in chapter 5) help in establishing the input to the quality house.

The quality house requires the use of brainstorming, cause-and-effect analysis, block diagram creation, process flowcharting, designed experiments, and testing techniques to develop the matrix. The matrix analysis then helps to analyze the results to formulate action plans. Knowledge of the use of these tools helps achieve the correct requirements and measures to use to develop the service process. Once the house is developed, you will be able to deploy the requirements for the service to your entire organization. Everyone will need to develop their services and to provide these services consistently to internal and external customers. In our experience, you need to use most of these tools to successfully complete the house of quality and provide maximum benefits for the organization.

The completion of the quality house will help you determine the key characteristics of the service and the measures to apply so you can evaluate whether the output will meet customers' needs. We hope that the examples used in this book are helpful to the readers in applying the approaches to their service or product applications. To be competitive in today's world market, you need to decipher the customers' differing needs and apply the input of customers throughout your organization to achieve services that will meet their needs. This may require that you develop several types of services to serve the entire market, one for each segment with different needs. We hope that you develop a matrix that is useful to the entire organization and provides the dynamics to keep all personnel in tune with your chosen market and your customers' needs. The matrix by itself is a great tool for selecting the requirements and the measures for the process or product. If you use the entire quality house as intended, you obtain much more design information for the service process, such as interactions between one process step and another step in the flow.

In this approach, you are working on attributes based on true customer consequences that will provide satisfaction to the customer and capture more of the customer base. The more customers you attract, the more your sales will grow. Therefore, the connection is to know the market and customer base well enough to meet customer needs and increase sales. With the identification of key processes and parameters that satisfy customers, the organization becomes more efficient and effective. This combination leads to more profit from increased sales and even economies of scale. Knowledge of key processes and parameters lead to process controls that will stabilize your profitability. This leads to an increase in return on capital employed (ROCE).[1] Every project that we have been involved with using this approach has provided a minimum of $100,000 savings to the bottom line.

This process will bring rewards to the organization if it is properly developed. Many of the Six Sigma projects (refer to appendix H for explanation) require us to focus on customer needs and to work only on projects that will provide an impact to the bottom line of the organization. To positively affect the organization, we need to assure that we are focusing on a balance in measures that will link our responses to key processes and incorporate metrics for success. You must align the projects to the strategy of the corporation and balance differing customer needs. One way to increase this focus is to evaluate the projects based on the ROCE for the service provided. The value is ROCE, the net profit increase after taxes divided by the capital employed. Therefore, if we produce more with the same capital or increase our sales based on more customer satisfaction with the same capital, our return on that capital will increase.

This book is a good reference for those perusing the road of lean concepts and Six Sigma processes in the service industries. These programs must start with knowledge of the customers' needs and the measures required for the process to exceed the customers' expectations and for the customers to become delighted with the service.

ENDNOTE

1. Some readers will be more familiar with return on investment (ROI), a similar concept.

Appendix A

Cause-and-Effect (Fishbone) Diagram

We can use this tool to assess conformance to customer requirements or to develop the possible requirements to meet the customer's needs. A cause-and-effect diagram represents the relationships between a given effect and its potential causes. We draw the cause-and-effect diagrams to sort out and relate the interactions among the factors affecting a process. A well-detailed cause-and-effect diagram will take the shape of a fishbone, hence its alias.

The procedure is:

1. Define the problem (effect) clearly and objectively.
2. Define the major categories of the possible causes. Use generic branches when possible.
3. The factors that we may consider are:
   - Information systems
   - Dollars
   - Measurements
   - Mother nature
   - People
   - Methods
   - Materials
   - Hardware

4. Begin to construct the diagram, defining the effect in a box at the right and positioning major categories as feeders to the effect box.
5. Brainstorm possible causes within the major categories and position these to feed into the related categories.
6. Analyze each cause to focus in on more specific causes.
7. Identify and circle the likely and actionable root causes.
8. Gather data to verify the most likely root causes. A Pareto diagram is a good way to display this data.

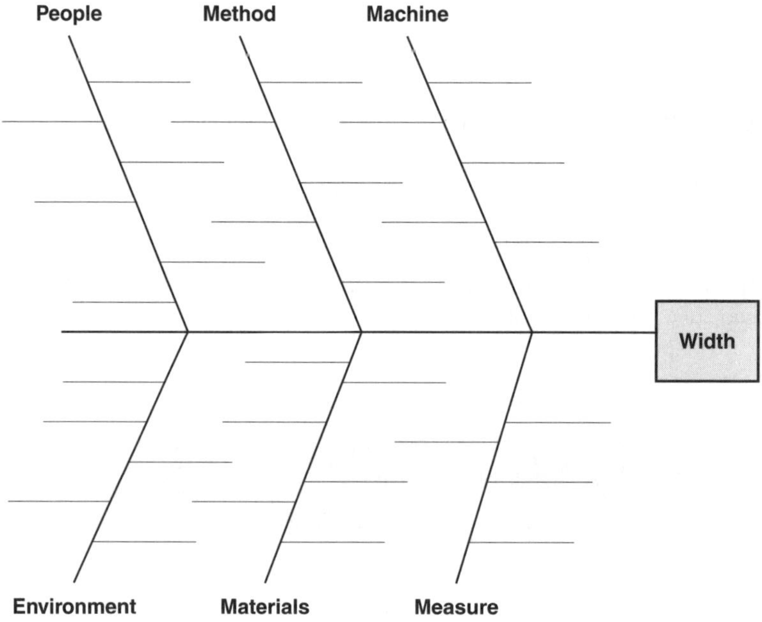

Appendix B

Designed Experiments

The following are some basic steps to take to develop a designed experiment to learn more about a process. There are many books written on the subject that will cover the detail required to perform an experiment. The outline or sequence below establishes the process. It is not as simple as the outline describes, but the steps will show you what has to be completed.

Designed experimentation process steps:

1. Choose the process that must be understood and possibly improved.
2. Develop the key process X factors, inputs for the process to perform to the customer's requirements. A team is best in the selection process.
3. Establish the levels to set for the X factors that will cover the output Y factors.
4. Understand and control the noise factors to the process in some manner, that is, block, hold constant, or randomize.
5. Verify the output Y factor that addresses the customer's needs.
6. Establish and design the experiment.
7. Run the experiment.
8. Evaluate the results of the experiment.

9. If the results show possible multifactor affects, run additional experiments.
10. Once the experiments are completed, you will have the key factors and levels that will deliver to the customer's needs.

Appendix C

Tree Diagram

The tree diagram uses a systematic approach to define a hierarchy of needs and objectives or characteristics and goals. The tree diagram will help in exploring possible causes of problems, to define specific tasks to reach higher goals, and to translate underdefined needs into operational characteristics.

The procedure for tree diagram development is:

1. State the problem.
2. Generate all possible tasks.
3. Construct the tree diagram.
    - Place the central problem to the left of the chart.
    - Find the ideas that are most closely related to the problem statement.
    - Place the ideas immediately to the right of the central problem.
    - Focus on the central problem and repeat the task generation steps until all the ideas are exhausted.
    - Review the tree diagram for obvious gaps in sequence or logic.
    - Review the tree diagram with other groups for comments and recommendations.

Example:

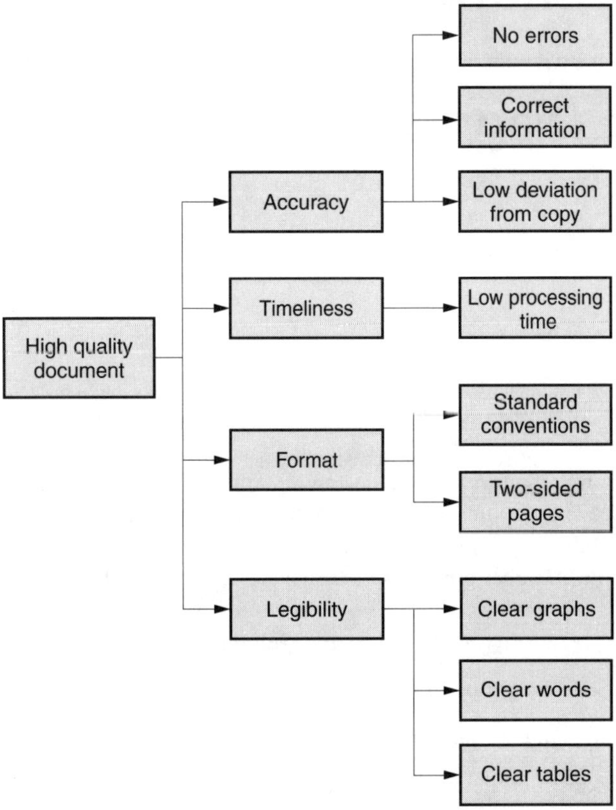
High quality document
Accuracy
Timeliness
Format
Legibility
No errors
Correct information
Low deviation from copy
Low processing time
Standard conventions
Two-sided pages
Clear graphs
Clear words
Clear tables

Appendix D

Benchmarking

Benchmarking measures your processes against those of recognized leaders in the process. It helps develop priorities to improve the process.

The procedure is generally as follows:

1. Determine what processes to benchmark. They should be key processes or characteristics of the process.
2. Determine whom to benchmark. Companies, organizations, or groups.
3. Determine the benchmarks: the measures, contacts, and data to be collected.
4. For each benchmark identified, determine the best-in-class target to review.
5. Requirements are based on both customer needs and benchmark targets.

Appendix E

Block Diagrams

Block diagrams help to develop a common understanding at a high level of how the process is currently or is required to operate and how major work groups within the process interact or interface with outside organizations. These diagrams trace the various paths that materials and information follow between inputs from the suppliers and the final outputs. The diagrams include blocks of activities required.

The process for creating a block diagram is:

1. Define the purpose and boundaries of the process.
2. Draw a box containing columns for each major work group within the process and then list the customers and suppliers external to the process.
3. For each input to the process, identify the supplier.
4. For each activity defined, determine the output it produces, the activity or customer who receives the output, and the individual or group that performs the activity.
5. Label each new activity box and continue generating information or workflows until all processes are connected together.
6. Verify the members of each work group that are reflected by the block.

Example: This figure shows a block diagram for a service of producing a document for the customer.

Purpose: The purpose of the process is to produce and distribute a document for the internal customer.

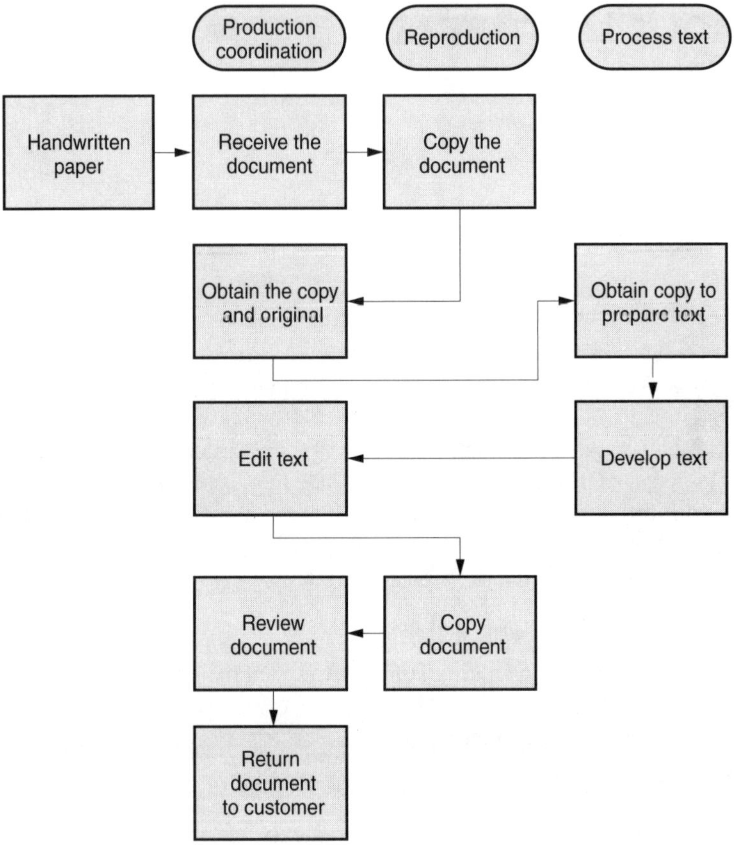

Appendix F

The Malcolm Baldrige National Quality Award Process

The service industries, including hospitals and schools, have been included in this process since 2000. The process is a set of seven criteria that organizations use to run their business, no matter what type of business is being performed by the organization. More information about the process can be obtained from the National Institute of Standards and Technology, based in Maryland.

The seven criteria are:

1. The leadership system that is used to manage and lead the organization.
2. The strategic planning process that exists within the organization to lead and plan the future for the short term of one year and then the long term of up to five years.
3. The customer and market knowledge process to determine the customer base, the customer satisfaction and dissatisfaction level, and the marketplace trends and needs.
4. The measurement system that is in place to determine the customer, financial, and operating parameters that are important to the organization and the customers.
5. The human resource needs of the organization to plan work and support employee growth and well-being.

6. The design and implementation of the processes that are needed for the organization to produce and deliver the products or services that are needed by the marketplace.
7. The results of customer satisfaction, financial, and operational requirements.

The important items of the Baldrige process are the linkages in the criteria. The first three criteria will link together to set the direction for the organization. The leadership system must take the input from the marketplace and customers to develop the strategy for the organization in category two.

The measurement system must maintain the measures that will determine the customer satisfaction level, marketplace trends, and the financial condition of the organization. The measures must be in place to monitor the key processes that will deliver the service to the customers and the design process to develop the key processes to new or changing needs of the customer. The measurement system must be capable of monitoring the metrics with the precision and accuracy required by the parameters. This category will link to all other categories to ensure that the proper measures are developed and the data are provided to those who must have the information to make decisions about the key processes that are in place.

Category five and six should link to each other to provide the skilled employees with the means to develop and monitor the key processes and provide the performance to the process so the customers are satisfied. Category seven will link the results to most other categories to tie the measures selected in these categories to the results of the organization performance.

The criteria require that the organization look at the customers and market to assure that the knowledge is obtained to concentrate on the true customer needs and the key processes that must be maintained to fulfill their needs. Category three is the area that addresses the customer and market, which provides guidance on the need for listening posts and customer input to address the potential changes in the market and the current and future needs of the customers. This can best be accomplished using the voice of the customer process and the QFD process. The process discussed in our book will provide the methods to achieve the results that will meet the intent of the criteria in this category. We then use this information in the design and development process to provide services that will meet the needs and consequences that are determined through the voice of the customer.

Appendix G

ANSI/ISO/ASQ Q9001-2000 and ISO/TS 16949

The international standard for quality for the general industry, including service organizations, is covered by quality systems and practices in the ANSI/ISO/ASQ Q9001-2000 standard. The automotive industry has developed its own standard, named ISO/TS 16949, that follows the points of ANSI/ISO/ASQ Q9001-2000 with some additional requirements for the auto industry. The aerospace industry completed the same international standards with AS9100 and the communication industry with TL 9000.

The international standards have a series of elements that are guidelines to a good basic quality system for all industries, with the exception of the industry-specific standards. The new standard for ANSI/ISO/ASQ Q9001-2000 has eight major areas with elements listed for these areas. The areas are:

1. Scope (of the standard)
2. Normative references
3. Terms and definitions
4. Quality management system
5. Management responsibility
    - Quality manual
    - Quality representative appointment
    - Documentation and control

6. Resource management
   - Facilities
   - Training
   - Knowledge and skills
7. Product realization
   - Purchasing
   - Operations control
   - Design and development
8. Measurement, analysis and improvement
   - Customer satisfaction
   - Internal audit
   - Control of nonconforming product
   - Corrective action

The majority of the standards follow the above format to provide a guide for the quality system. The elements have several subelements for each section to be fulfilled for the system. You need to review approximately 145 different elements for the system to be effective.

The element of product realization covers the need to obtain customer needs to develop the processes, which will provide the services to meet the customer's needs and therefore satisfy the customer. In the quality management system process description, the customer satisfaction level for the current customers needs to be identified. The satisfaction and dissatisfaction feedback from the customer is required. The results of the process are improved through a prevention system that will maintain and improve upon customer satisfaction.

Appendix H

The Six Sigma Process

The Six Sigma overview provided here will inform the reader of the process and how it must focus on the customer's requirements in order to develop the "critical to quality" characteristics for the key processes.

Six Sigma is the evaluation of the business process improvement requirements to meet or exceed customer requirements, improve productivity, and thus increase profitability. The concepts and methods of Six Sigma focus on the customer, process mapping/evaluation, and eliminating variation within the processes. The methods help us with problem-solving tools, measure the impact of process performance, and then identify the bottom-line results using breakthrough improvements.

This Six Sigma approach can apply to all types and sizes of organizations. This approach also applies to every aspect of products, services, departmental functions, hardware, software, or production and design processes.

Motorola originally created and implemented the Six Sigma process in the early 1980s. This concept has spread to many different organizations after Allied Signal, General Electric, and ABB adopted the concept.

The Six Sigma process will focus on processes (not just the product), the measures of the process, the customer, and the organization. We differentiate this process from other quality activities because it does focus on the customer, process, and measures of performance. Six Sigma is a different philosophy, a method of using available tools, a required commitment from management, and an attitude to want to succeed and be different. We plan the Six Sigma process to be successful in reducing variation, costs, and improving profitability. The Six Sigma process should begin with the executive team using the strategic planning process to align the activities of Six

Sigma to the business needs and customer needs and become more competitive in the market place.

We typically teach the Six Sigma process over a four- to five-month period of training, application, and learning on the philosophies, tools to use, and lean operation concepts. There are four full weeks of training/learning followed by three weeks in between each week of training for the application of the tools on an actual problem.

Six Sigma heads a process toward the level of 3.4 defects per million operations or units, which gets us close to zero defects to the customer. Six Sigma addresses process defects, wasted time, and throughput of product or service. Since the focus is on the customer and the critical to quality characteristics, the voice of the customer and the quality function deployment process we have outlined in this book will support the Six Sigma process.

Appendix I

Answers to Chapter Exercises

CHAPTER 3

1.

Attributes / Consequences	Pastries are offered	Quiet atmosphere	Tables available	Many flavors of coffee	Competitive prices	Quick service	Friendly service	Computers available to rent
Coffee tastes good								
I can get my coffee quickly								
Located near my home								
My friends go there								
I can study there								
I can socialize there								

2. This consumer would chose the Acme brand based on its sum of weighted ratings being highest, using the compensatory method of decision making.

Consequences	Importance Rating	Acme		Bell		Class	
		Rating	Weighted Rating	Rating	Weighted Rating	Rating	Weighted Rating
Delivered overnight	10	10	100	2	20	7	70
Delivered the day I want	10	4	40	6	60	4	40
No damage	8	10	80	8	64	4	32
Within budget	5	5	25	8	40	10	50
Sum of weighted ratings			245		184		192

CHAPTER 4

1. The answers to this question will vary with the individual reader. The answer below represents an example only.

   What comes to mind when you think of having pizza delivered?

   What do you look for when you have pizza delivered?

   What is important to you in pizza delivery?

   What pizza delivery companies can you name?

   From what companies do you order pizza?

   Tell me about the best pizza delivery service you ever had.

   Tell me about the worst pizza delivery service you ever had.

   When do you usually have pizza delivered?

   What happens when you get bad pizza delivery?

Attributes / Consequences	Crust type	Many topping choices	Delivery speed	Not put on hold	Fresh toppings	Sauce flavor	Amount of cheese	Amount of toppings	Operating hours	Ordering process	Amount of sauce
The pizza tastes good											
My order is taken quickly											
Delivery is quick											
I can get my favorite toppings											
The pizza is hot when I get it											
I can order when I want											
I save money											
The crust is crispy											
The cheese doesn't stick to the box											
The dough is cut all the way through											
The pizza is cooked through											
The sauce covers the dough											
The pizza is not greasy											
I get enough cheese											
I get enough toppings											

CHAPTER 5

1. The answers to this question will vary with the individual reader. The answer below represents an example only.

   Find the consequence in the list below that is most important to you. Assign it ten (10) points. Then assign from zero (0) to ten (10) points to the other consequences to indicate how important they are to you in comparison to the one that is most important. You may assign the same number of points to more than one consequence.

   ______ The pizza tastes good.

   ______ My order is taken quickly.

   ______ Delivery is quick.

   ______ I can get my favorite toppings.

   ______ The pizza is hot when I get it.

   ______ I can order when I want.

   ______ I save money.

   ______ The crust is crispy.

   ______ The cheese doesn't stick to the box.

   ______ The dough is cut all the way through.

   ______ The pizza is cooked through.

   ______ The sauce covers the dough.

   ______ The pizza is not greasy.

   ______ I get enough cheese.

   ______ I get enough toppings.

CHAPTER 6

Please rate how well each of the brands below do on delivering pizza to you in each of the areas listed below. Circle the number below that best indicates how well you feel we satisfy each of the consequences. Use a scale of:

1 = Strongly disagree

2 = Disagree

3 = Neutral

4 = Agree

5 = Strongly agree

	Papa John's	Pizza Hut	Domino's
The pizza tastes good	1 2 3 4 5	1 2 3 4 5	1 2 3 4 5
My order is taken quickly	1 2 3 4 5	1 2 3 4 5	1 2 3 4 5
Delivery is quick	1 2 3 4 5	1 2 3 4 5	1 2 3 4 5
I can get my favorite toppings	1 2 3 4 5	1 2 3 4 5	1 2 3 4 5
The pizza is hot when I get it	1 2 3 4 5	1 2 3 4 5	1 2 3 4 5
I can order when I want	1 2 3 4 5	1 2 3 4 5	1 2 3 4 5
I save money	1 2 3 4 5	1 2 3 4 5	1 2 3 4 5
The crust is crispy	1 2 3 4 5	1 2 3 4 5	1 2 3 4 5
The cheese doesn't stick to the box	1 2 3 4 5	1 2 3 4 5	1 2 3 4 5
The dough is cut all the way through	1 2 3 4 5	1 2 3 4 5	1 2 3 4 5
The pizza is cooked through	1 2 3 4 5	1 2 3 4 5	1 2 3 4 5
The sauce covers the dough	1 2 3 4 5	1 2 3 4 5	1 2 3 4 5
The pizza is not greasy	1 2 3 4 5	1 2 3 4 5	1 2 3 4 5
I get enough cheese	1 2 3 4 5	1 2 3 4 5	1 2 3 4 5
I get enough toppings	1 2 3 4 5	1 2 3 4 5	1 2 3 4 5
Overall, I am satisfied with this company's pizza delivery	1 2 3 4 5	1 2 3 4 5	1 2 3 4 5

CHAPTER 7

1. Wine cooler customer needs.

   The wine cooler exercise takes into consideration the analysis of the consequences and the attributes for the customer. If the student takes a look at the information in chapter 3, they will recognize that the consequences were obtained from the attributes and therefore one could view this problem two different ways.

   List the consequences from the attribute data. The student will need to contact female users of wine or wine coolers to check on the prioritization or ranking of the attributes and the consequences. The student could create their own ranking based on past experience or observations from knowledge gained when experiencing wine coolers themselves or as noted with others purchasing the drink.

Consequences	Weight
High quality	8
Less filling	7
Refreshing	9
Consume less	6
Quenches thirst	10
Feminine	4

   If the consequences are used, the data may look like the following:

Attribute	Weight
Carbonated	9
Crisp	9
Expensive	8
Attractive label	4
Curved bottle	4
Low alcohol	6
Small size	6

2. Good tasting coffee.

   The customer attributes and consequences are obtained from a survey of coffee drinkers. The student needs to establish a sample size to take for good tasting coffee. The sample will have to be taken from present coffee drinkers and rank-ordered to the customer attributes from the customer base that is interviewed.

   Suggested results from the survey are:

Attributes	Weight
Brand coffee selection	10
Type of coffee selection	10
Type of condiments	6
Cream	6
Sugar	4
Hot	9
Good taste	9
Size cup selection	8
Value	7

CHAPTER 8

1. The wine cooler matrix development follows.

	Weight	Fermentation	Grape type	Recipe	Mixing	Aging	Bottle	Package	Weight	Optional
High quality	8	9	9	3	9	9	1		9	Carbonated
Less filling	7			1	9	3	3		9	Crisp
Refreshing	9	3	3	9	9	1	1		8	Expensive
Consume less	6		3	3	3	1	9	3	4	Attractive label
Quench thirst	10	3	3	3	9				4	Low alcohol
Feminine	1					3	9	9	6	Small size
Value		10 days	Soft	21	15 hours	2 years	Curved	Small		

2. Good tasting coffee matrix development.

	Weight	Bean type	Bean grind	Water quality	Water temperature	Fresh cream	Sugar quality	Blend type	Cup type
Coffee brand selection	10	9	1						
Coffee type selection	10	9	9	1				3	
Hot	9				9				9
Good taste	9	9	9	9	3	9	9	9	
Condiments	6					9	9		
Cream	6					9			
Sugar	4						9		
Size cup selection	8								9
Coffee value	7	3	9	3	9				9
Value		Columbia	High	Good	150°F	Pull date	Fair	Medium	Large

CHAPTER 9

1. Customer competitive analysis of our service to meet their needs is obtained during the interviewing process, by survey questionnaire, or by focus group process. The specific ways to obtain this analysis are to show the customer the competitive service, have them experience the service themselves, or ask if they have experienced the competitive service. If the technical competitive analysis is to be obtained, then the technical team must actually test and experience all the competitive services that are provided.

   Some questions that may be asked of the customers to obtain this information are: Have you obtained and experienced this service from other organizations? If so, who? How was your experience compared to our service?

2. If the competition is better than our organization or company, then we need to verify how the service is being provided and determine what it will take for us to compete. If the competition is not as good as our organization, then the organization must maintain its position and keep the service available.

3. The following is the matrix to cover the shipping process. The answers are based on your experience, and substantiating evidence.

		Auto sort	Air ship	Surface delivery	Hand carry	Hand sort	Hand delivery			Customer analysis 1 2 3 4 5
Fast delivery										X □ ○ ◉ ★
Cost of delivery										X □ ○ ◉ ★
No damage										○ □ X ◉ ★
Technical analysis same symbols	1 2 3 4 5	□ ◉ ○ □ ★ X	X ○ □ ★ ◉	★ □ ○ ◉ X	X □ ★ ◉ ○	★ □ ○ ◉ X	○ ◉ X □ ★			

X = UPS   □ = DHL   ○ = FedEx   ◉ = USPS   ★ = Us

CHAPTER 10

1. The matrix below provides the answers to the weather resistant product for the plastic part and the process correlations as noted by the author.

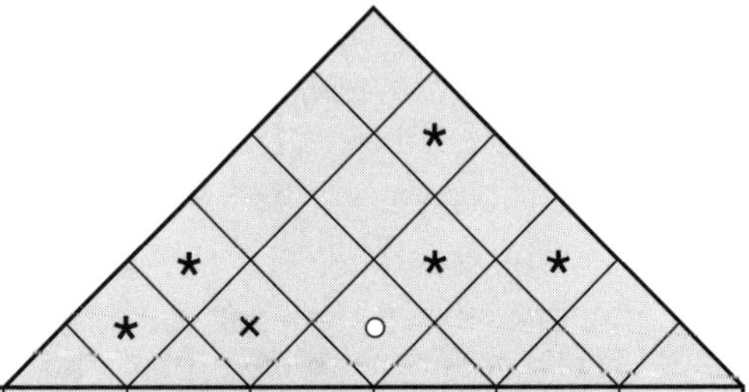

	Weight	Plastic type	Compound type	Forming process	Cooling process	Mixing process	Moisture control
No discoloring	10						
Temperature range	8						
Humidity range	5						
Vibration range	8						
Rain	9						
Value							

CHAPTER 11

The matrix below shows the values added to the bottom of the matrix with added indicators that might be better to use for the analysis of the performance of the doctor's office to meet the needs of the customer scheduling an appointment.

Customer consequences \ Technical requirements	Weight	System available	Care available	Scheduler speed	Doctor training	Doctor staff size	Scheduler accuracy	Scheduler flexibility	Doctor flexibility	System capability	Operator training	System speed	Training process	Screening process	Complaints
Time to appointment	8	⊙	⊙	⊙		⊙	⊙	⊙	⊙	⊙					10
Choice of days	9	⊙	⊙		⊙	⊙	⊙	⊙	⊙	⊙					5
Choice of times	5	⊙	⊙		⊙	⊙	⊙	⊙	⊙	⊙					20
Short time to schedule	9	△	⊙		⊙	⊙	⊙	⊙	⊙	⊙		⊙			15
Criticalness of visit determined	10										⊙		⊙	⊙	3
Appointment made without interruption	5	⊙	⊙	○			⊙	⊙	⊙	⊙	⊙	⊙		⊙	4
Appointment time kept	8	△			○	⊙	⊙	△	⊙	⊙	⊙			⊙	5
All questions answered	9										⊙		⊙		3
Insurance claims processed	8	○									⊙		⊙		4
Insurance coverage recognized	10										△		⊙	⊙	7
Value position		↓	↓	↑	↑	↑	↑	10 sec. ○	↑	↑	↑	↓	↑	↑	
Weight		284	324	87	231	351	396	332	396	390	126	333	297	250	
Value		5 sec.	2 days	5 sec.	Max.	Max.	100%	100%	100%	5 sec.	All	Completed	Completed	100%	

CHAPTER 12

1. The following matrices show the first room and how the output is related to the input of the second room with the ceiling filled out for the room.

	Weight by customer	Linen change process	Cleaning bath process	Room prep process	Carpet	Furniture	Lighting and TV
Bed made	9	⊙					
Clean bathroom	10		⊙	○			
Vacuumed	8		○	⊙	⊙		
Dusted	6			⊙		○	
Lighting	6			⊙			⊙
Coffee and so on	4			⊙			
Weight		81	114	216	72	108	54

Take the output numbers from the first room and divide them by 10 to obtain the input priority to the second room.

	Weight by customer	Folded linens applied	Bathroom cleaning process	Tables and chair position	Vacuuming process	Furniture dusting and layout	Appliance layout and cleanliness
Linen change process	8.1	⊙					
Clean bath process	11.4		⊙				
Room prep process	21.6		○	⊙	⊙	⊙	
Carpet	7.2				⊙	○	
Furniture	10.8			⊙		⊙	
Lighting and TV	5.4			⊙			⊙
Weight		72.9	168.4	340.2	259.2	313.2	48.6

2. The doctor's office can have two more rooms from the original planning matrix and the inputs follow.

   To room number three:

   System requirements
   Scheduler requirements
   Doctor's experience
   Staffing system
   Operator experience

   To room number four:

   System specification
   Scheduler training requirements
   Doctor's educational requirements
   The staffing requirements
   System specification for staff loading
   Operator hiring requirements
   Operator training

Additional References

Akao, Yoji, ed. *Quality Function Deployment: Integrating Customer Requirements into Product Design.* Cambridge, MA: Productivity Press, 1990.

Allen, Derek R., and Tanniru R. Rao. *Analysis of Customer Satisfaction Data.* Milwaukee: ASQ Quality Press, 2000.

Anderson, Mark, and Patrick Whitcomb. *DOE Simplified.*Portland, OR: Productivity, Inc., 2000.

Ang, David S., and Charles I. Hegji. "Quality Costs and Profits." *Southern Business Review* 23, no. 2 (1997): 1–10.

AT&T. *Process Quality Management and Improvement Guidelines.* Indianapolis: AT&T Customer Information Center, 1987.

Barrentine, Larry B. *An Introduction to Design of Experiments: A Simplified Approach.* Milwaukee: ASQ Quality Press, 1999.

Bossert, James L. *Quality Function Deployment: A Practitioner's Approach.* Milwaukee: ASQC Quality Press, 1991.

Box, George, William Gordon Hunter, and Stuart Hunter. *Statistics for Experimenters.* New York: John Wiley & Sons, 1978.

Burke, Eve, Jack M. Kloeber, Jr., and Richard F. Dekro. "Using and Abusing QFD Scores." *Quality Engineering* 15, no. 1 (2002–03).

Chan, Lai-Kow, and Ming-Lu Wu. "Quality Function Deployment: A Comprehensive Review of Its Concepts and Methods." *Quality Engineering Journal* 15, no. 1 (2002–03).

Cohen, Lou, and Louis Cohen. *Quality Function Deployment.* New York: Prentice Hall, 1995.

Day, Ronald G. *Quality Function Deployment: Linking a Company with Its Customers.* Milwaukee: ASQC Quality Press, 1993.

Gale, Bradley T. *Managing Customer Value: Creating Quality and Service that Customers Can See.* New York: The Free Press, 1994.

Griffin, Abbie, and John R. Hauser. "The Voice of the Customer." *Marketing Science Institute*. Working paper report number 92-106, 1992.

Henderson, Gary W. "Ben & Jerry's Recipe." *Customer Service Management* (Nov/Dec 1999).

King, Bob. *Better Designs in Half the Time: Implementing QFD Quality Function Deployment in America.* Methuen, MA: GOAL/QPC, 1989.

Martilla, John A., and John C. James. "Importance–Performance Analysis," *Journal of Marketing* 41, no. 1 (1977): 77–79.

Moen, Ronald, Thomas Nolan, and Lloyd Provost. *Improving Quality through Planned Experimentation.* New York: McGraw-Hill, 1991.

Naumann, Earl. *Creating Customer Value: The Path to Sustainable Competitive Advantage.* Cincinnati, OH: Thomson Executive Press, 1995.

Parasuraman, A., Valarie A. Zeithaml, and Leonard L. Berry. "Moving Forward in Service Quality Research: Measuring Different Customer-Expectation Levels, Comparing Alternative Scales, and Examining the Performance–Behavioral Intentions Link." *Marketing Science Institute.* Working paper report number 94-114, 1994.

———. "SERVQUAL: A Multiple-Item Scale for Measuring Consumer Perceptions of Service Quality." *Journal of Retailing* 64, no. 1 (1988): 12–40.

ReVelle, Jack B., John W. Moran, and Charles A. Cox. *The QFD Handbook.* New York: John Wiley & Sons, 1998.

Robinson, G. K. *Practical Strategies for Experimenting.* New York: John Wiley & Sons, 2000.

Ross, Phillip. *Taguchi Techniques for Quality Engineering.* New York: McGraw-Hill, 1988.

Tatikonda, Lakshmi, and Rao J. Tatikonda. "Measuring and Reporting the Cost of Quality." *Production and Inventory Management Journal* 37, no. 2 (1996): 1–8.

Woodruff, Robert B., and Sarah F. Gardial. *Know Your Customer: New Approaches to Understanding Customer Value and Satisfaction.* Cambridge, MA: Blackwell Publishers, 1996.

Index

A

ABB, 195
action goals, 123
action plans, 123
affinity diagram, 32
Akao, Yoji, 2, 10
    model of matrix of matrices, 13
Allied Signal, 195
American Customer Satisfaction Index (ACSI), 3
    scores, 3
American Society for Quality (ASQ), 3
anchored scale, 43
ANSI/ISO/ASQ Q9001-2000, 193–94
    major areas, 193–94
AS9100, 10, 193
attribute/consequence grid, 19–20, 23
    relationships, 19–20
attributes, 11, 18–20
    rating, 11
    service, 26
    understanding differences, 31

B

basics of measurement, 39–41
benchmarking, 119, 187
    procedure, 187
Better Business Bureau, 172
block diagrams, 123–24, 189–90
    creation process, 189–90
    example, 190
    purpose, 190
brainstorming process, 61, 67
    phases of, 61
    phases of, clarification, 61
    phases of, generation, 61
    rules, 61
brand positioning, 148–50

C

cause-and-effect analysis process, 67
cause-and-effect diagram, 5, 62, 66–69, 181–82
    example, 160
    major categories, 66–67
cause-and-effect method, 120
cause-and-effect process, 67
CFI Group, 3
cluster analysis, 22, 33, 147–48
compensatory decision-making model, 20–22
competitive advantage, 128
competitive analysis, 11, 48
    example, 156–60
    service, 11
competitive comparisons, 48–50, 96
competitive evaluation, 48
competitive grid, 143
    example, 157–59
competitive profile, 49, 142
    visual, 49
competitive ratings, 48
conceptual block diagrams, 123–24
conceptual design process, 123–24
consequences, 11, 18–22, 26
    adding missing, 34
    basic, 29–30, 39, 40
    customer, 11
    cutting-edge, 30
    establishing goals, 101
    excitement, 30–31
    exemplar, 32–33
    finding missing, 34

identifying, 31
other sources, 31
performance, 28–29, 145
price, 145
understanding differences, 31
consumer segments, 22
correlation analysis, 108–10
cost of quality, 170–71
cost of quality analysis, 170–71
cost savings, 170–71
customer, 11
customer competitive assessment, 96–97
customer complaints column, 116–18
customer consequence, 11
customer importance rating, 38–39
customer input process, 12
customer, lifetime value, 173
customer loyalty, 172–73
customer matrix 128
customer relationship management (CRM), 172–73
customer requirements, developmental process for technical information matrix, 64–66
customer retention, 171–72
customer retention, rate, 172
customer satisfaction, 171, 178
customer sort, 32–33
customer value map, 144–45
customer voice, 11, 26, 178
example, 156
importance, 60
organizing, 32–33
process, 67, 108
customer weighted input, 118
cycle time, 171
cycle time, reduction, 171

D

data collection process, 99
data validity, 51–52
data verification, 51–52
delighters, 116–17
design concepts, 108
design process, 108, 123–24
design requirements, correlations, 108
design team, 60
designed experiments, 183–84
process steps, 183–84
diagram, key block, 108
diagram, tree, 62–66, 185–86
procedure for, 185–86
diagrams, block, 123–24, 189–90
creation process, 189–90
example, 190
purpose, 190
diagrams, cause-and-effect, 5, 62, 66–69, 181–82
example, 160
major categories, 66–67
diagrams, conceptual block, 123–24
diagrams, relationship, 5
directions of improvement, 119–21
row, 117
dissatisfiers, 116
doctor's office example, 23, 35, 44–45, 53–55, 69–76, 90–93, 101–5, 113, 128–29, 135–36, 150–52

E

exercises, 24, 35–36, 45, 55, 77, 93, 105, 114, 130, 137, 152

F

fishbone diagram (*see* cause and effect diagram)
Florida Power and Light, 4
focus groups, 26, 27–28
advantage, of, 27
challenges, of, 28
facilitator, 27
moderator, 27–28

G

Gale, Bradley T., 146
gaps, 49–50, 142
General Electric, 195

H

house of quality (*see* quality house)
hows (*see* technical requirements)

I

importance analysis, example, 156–60
importance scales, 41–44
anchored, 43
constant sum, 43
itemized rating, 42
rank order, 41
importance–performance grid, 127, 142–44, 150
example, 165
improvement ratio, 123
interview process, 11
interviewer, 26
interviews, 26–27
ISO 16949:2000, 10
ISO 9001:2000, 10
ISO/TS 16949, 193

J

Japanese Deming Prize, 4

K

Kano model, 28–31, 38, 116
key block diagram, 108
key process parameters, 132–37

L

Likert scale, 48
Likert-type scale, 48
Loyola University New Orleans, 178

M

Malcom Baldrige National Quality Process, 191–92
  criteria, 191–92
  important items, 192
market segmentation, 147–48, 178
  importance of, 150
marketing and sales analysis, 101
marketing priorities and strategies, example, 165
matrix, customer, 128
matrix log, customer design, 66–69
matrix, parts, 132
matrix, process, 132
matrix, technical, 120–21
matrix, technical correlation, 108
measurements scales, 39–41
  metric, 40
    interval scale, 40
    ratio scale, 40
  non-metric, 40
    nominal scales, 40–41
    ordinal scales, 40
measures, development 86–87
Mizuno, Shigeru, 2
Motorola, 195
mystery shopper, 96, 97, 98
  example, 160

N

National Institute of Standards and Technology (NIST), 191

O

operational targets, example, 160
optimal levels, 87–88
  setting, 87–88
  value, 87–88

P

parts matrix, 132
parts parameters, 134–35
performance consequence, 145
plot, 49
positioning map, 148, 150
price consequence, 145
priority column, 117–19
probing, 26, 27
  techniques, 23
process, design, 123–24
process development, example, 163
process matrix, 132
process performance, 112
process specifications, 133–34
product parameters, 194
product realization, 194
profits, 174
Pugh analysis, 123–24
  steps for, 123–24
Pugh concept, 124
Pugh, Stuart, 123

Q

QFD house (see quality house)
quality function deployment (QFD), 2, 3, 10, 170
  advantages, 2
  founder, 10
  four phases, 132
  process, 2, 10, 12, 117, 178
    benefits of, 80
  results, 170
  tool, 10
quality house, 12–13, 60, 80–81, 84, 97–99, 120, 132, 135, 178
  development, 69
  example, 160
  linkage, 80
  models, 13
    ASI phase, 13
    clausing model, 13
    four phase, 13
  placement, 52
  roof, 108–13
  technical correlations, roof, 108–13
  technical matrix, 120–21
    considerations, 121

R

ranking, 11
  needs and expectations, 11
rating, customer importance 38

relationship diagrams, 5
relationship matrix, 84, 104
symbols, 84–85
relationships, 84
analysis, 119
determination, 81–85
linkage, 83–85
weighting, 84
relative performance, 145
relative price, 145
resource allocations, 142–44
prioritizing, 142–44
retention rate, 172
return on capital employed (ROCE), 180

S

sales improvement, 122
action goals, 123
action plans, 123
column, 122–24
goals, 122–23
ratio, 123
sales, increased, 174
sales points, 97, 101
satisfiers, 116
scales, 39–41
importance, 41–44
anchored, 43
constant sum, 43
itemized rating, 42
rank order, 41
interval, 40
Likert, 48
measurement, 39–41
nominal, 40–41
ordinal, 40, 48
ratio, 40–41
segmentation map, 148
service industries, 3–4
customer satisfaction, 3
service organizations, 3
service process, 66
alternatives, 66
services, 3–4
QFD for, 4
Six Sigma, 195–96
concepts, 195
lean process, 6
methods, 195
tools, 5
training programs, 5
Six Sigma process, 5–6, 195–96
statistical tests, 40
metric, 40
non-metric, 40
strategic competitive advantage, 175
strategic tools, 13

T

target, 127–28
target directions, 120
target symbols, 120
target values, 119
technical characteristic, 60–77
technical comparisons, 98
technical competitive analysis, 88–89, 96–105
comparing, 99–101
differences, 88–89
technical competitive assessment, 89, 96
example, 160
technical competitive ratings, example, 160
technical correlation matrix, 108
technical evaluation, 98
technical feature, 120
technical information, organizing, 62–66
technical matrix, 120–21
analyzing, 86
technical requirements, 60–77, 80–93
correlations, 108–13
developmental process, 111
testing approaches, 109
determination, 81
example, 160–63
generating, 61–62
relationships, 120
relative importance, 125–26
relative importance ratings, 125
technical trade-offs, 108–9
example, 160
technical verification 99
Tennessee Technological University, 4
application of QFD, 4
testing routines, 98–99
TL 9000, 193
trade-off, example, 160
tree diagram, 5, 62–66, 185–86
example, 160
procedure for, 185–86
rules for success, 63
three layer, 62–63

U

U. S. Postal Service, 18
University of Michigan Business School, 3
University of Michigan Medical Center, 4

V

visual competitive profile, 49
voice of the customer (see customer voice)